12-16-63

The Royal Birds

The Royal Birds

LILLIAN GRACE PACA

illustrated by the author

ST MARTIN'S PRESS   NEW YORK

TO

my two Margarets

Author's Preface

THIS BOOK is written for People to read and enjoy. Scientists may be disappointed in it, even scornful, for it is designed for the layman who merely wants to know more about these elusive birds, the small intimate things, the family life, the legends, the stories. Swans live in two worlds, the world of Nature and the world of Romance; they do not lend themselves to the pages of a textbook.

So little is known about swans and practically nothing written. My bibliography is necessarily short and the list of individuals who have helped me, incredibly long.

Author's Preface

I am especially indebted to the British Broadcasting Company for supplying two original scripts of programs, and to Mr. Tony Soper, their naturalist, who has been my mainstay, providing me with encouragement as well as unusual data. The U.S. Department of the Interior, Fish and Wildlife Service also supplied much valuable information, while Mr. Kenton C. Lint and Mr. John A. Griswold of the San Diego and Philadelphia Zoos were very helpful, particularly on the subject of the Coscoroba swans. Sir Harry Howard, the Lord Mayor of Perth, Western Australia, kindly introduced me to Dr. S. L. Serventy of the Australian Wildlife Survey for information on the native Black Swans.

Mr. R. L. Cunningham of Woodinville, Washington State, not only contributed to the final chapter but checked and edited my script as well. I should also like to mention Mr. Peter Scott, Mr. Bruce Campbell, Mr. Chauncey Hyatt, Mr. Winston E. Banko, Mr. Richard E. Griffith, and the librarian of the Library Research Service of the *Encyclopaedia Britannica* in London, Mr. Fred Lexter of Abbotsbury, and Mrs. Harold Pope of Sydney, Australia. Dr. Lucy McLane of Stanford University furnished the beautiful translation of the Swan Riddle from the ancient Exeter Book.

Nature Magazine allowed me to use material, and I consulted the following books: A. C. Bent's *Life Histories of North American Wild Fowl* (Dover Publications, N.Y.); Francis H. Kortright's *Ducks, Geese and Swans of North America* (Stackpole Co., Harrisburg, Pa.); H. F. Witherby's *The Handbook of British Birds* (H. F. and G. Witherby, Ltd., London); and *Waterfowl of the World*, by Jean Delacour and Peter Scott (W. S. Heinman, N.Y.).

Many, many more have encouraged and helped me. I only wish I could give them all credit and thanks here.

LILLIAN GRACE PACA

Old English Terms to Describe Swans

COB	*The male swan*
PEN	*The female swan*
CYGNET	*The young swan*
GAME	*A flock of swans privately owned*
HERD	*A flock of wild swans*
HEIERY	*A nest or collection of nests*
SWANHERD	*A keeper of swans for a private owner*
SWAN-MASTER	*Royal swanherd*
BUSKING	*Position of raised wings when swimming*

Contents

The Royal Birds

❧ 1 ❧

The Royal Birds

ENGLAND is a land of rivers and lakes and rush-bordered pools, a land beloved of swans. In my childhood I was always fascinated by the great white birds, serenely aloof and elegant, princes and princesses of some fabulous fairyland. They were considered dangerous, I remember, but with the natural confidence of a child I held long conversations with them, conversations that were very real to me.

In the intervening years I traveled far from the swan-haunted island, but recently I journeyed back. Barely was the great liner tied to the dockside at Southampton when they came to greet me. Swimming in a long, perfectly spaced line down the dawn-clear water they came, their long necks erect, proud wings busked like snowy, wind-filled spinnaker sails. A truly royal welcome!

Very little is known about swans. It is strange that ornithologists have so neglected these most spectacular of our water birds. Poets have written countless romantic verses about them, and they are woven into many fantastic tales, but the home life of the swan family has remained unstudied and unwritten.

Yet swans in much their present form probably inhabited this earth long before Man. Fossils of a swan have been unearthed in the chalky soil of the Lower Cretaceous System beside remains of the then already declining race of dinosaurs and the upspringing winged creatures which were to evolve into the birds of today. The original birds were toothed and unfeathered, but they were advanced beyond the reptile form of the terrible flying pterodactyls. The swan bones discovered closely resemble those of the present-day Coscoroba, the swan-goose of South America. Though toothless and apparently feathered, that ancient swan may possibly have been the first of the true water birds.

Scientists rank swans very low in the scale of bird evolution, lower even than geese, their near relatives, for they have remained water birds. It is assumed that, since the original bird was an aquatic creature, the more his descendants are adapted to water the nearer they are to their primal ancestor—thus the lower they must perch on the family tree.

Nevertheless, swans are definitely aristocrats: the great Trumpeter of North America bears the impressive title of *Cygnus buccinator*, while the wild Whooper of Northern Europe is known as *Cygnus-cygnus-cygnus*, truly hyphenated and noble. They hold their heads high on their long necks at all times and have an intelligence equal to that of the raven, the wisest of birds, and a fidelity to mate and young admirable in any species.

Wild swans far outnumber the semitame, found on park lakes and rivers all over the world. But in Europe and America these wild birds nest far away in the uninhabited ends of the earth and fly so high on migration that all you know of their passing in the fall and in the spring is the faint measured beat of their great wings and the bugle-clear notes drifting down from the night sky as they journey toward their northern summer home or toward their southern winter refuge.

In the Northern Hemisphere there are six species of wild swans, seven if you include the semidomesticated Mute. The truly wild ones are the great Trumpeter, the smaller Whistler of the West, the mighty Whooper, the dainty Bewick's, the very beautiful Immutable of Europe, and the little-known Russian (Siberian) swan, which lives behind the Iron Curtain and is called Jankowski. South of the equator there are three distinct species: the magnificent Black of Australia, the curious Black-neck of South America, and, strangest of all, the Coscoroba, that extraordinary swan-goose of the Argentine, which is the link with the fossil swan of the chalk deposits.

These ten species of the genus called cygnus are distributed all over the world with the exception of the continent of Africa. Aloof and wary, disdainful of the earth-bound circle of Man, these wild ones are the undisputed monarchs of the air. They nest around the polar ice and in winter fly south to the temperate zone choosing remote and uninhabited places, where they scatter to rest and feed. Even when they are seen, they so much resemble the tame Mutes of the city parks that few people realize they are actually viewing those most romantic of all birds, the wild swans.

So unapproachable are they that, swimming on a mountain tarn, they seem as remote as the constellation of Cygnus the Swan, glittering far in the northern sky. No wonder the ancient Hindus spoke of the "Swan out of Time and Space."

The Mute, the swan we all know, is the royal bird of England that has been installed in parks and lakes all over the world. Rumor says it was introduced into England by Julius Caesar, but it is definitely a wild swan of Northern Europe and must certainly have been established in the island of Britain long before the Romans arrived. No doubt the invaders domesticated the big showy birds, and later rulers reserved them as royal gifts to be bestowed upon favored courtiers. It is not known when the stately swan was first designated as a bird-royal, but it is possible that the invading Danes of the early centuries already had this conception.

In Emsworth on the coast of Hampshire there is a record of a swan that joined the local herd in 1737, wearing around its neck a golden crown inscribed with the letters R.V.I.

(Regis Vivari Incola, or Royal Fishpond Dweller). Speculation is that it must have flown across the North Sea, for in 1776 another swan was reported on the coast of Norfolk wearing "a crown of silver inscribed with the arms of the King of Denmark."

The first known deed of a royal gift of a "Game of Swannes" is dated 1023, when the Danish conqueror King Canute bestowed certain lands in and around Abbotsbury in Dorset. The "Games and Flightes of Swannes" then resident on the waters of the Fleet were granted to his servant Orc "for his amiable fidelity and willing mind, so that he may have and perpetually possess the same as long as his life may continue and, when he shall perceive the dissolution of his body to be near, it shall be lawful for him to leave the same to his heir, whomsoever, in hereditary right forever."

This deed by King Canute can still be seen among the Melbury archives. Though the present landowner, Lord Illchester, is not a direct descendant of the Danish Orc, his family has cared for the swans for over five hundred years.

The birds still congregate at the celebrated swannery of Abbotsbury, which is open to the public during the summer months.

Edward IV seems to have been the first monarch to make a serious business of swan-keeping. During his reign complicated laws were enacted with a long list of penalties attached. A nesting place was called a heiery and was considered sacrosanct. The driving of a swan from a heiery warranted a year's imprisonment. Owners of swans were obliged to pay a license for each swanherd employed to protect their "games" and none but a registered swanherd might carry a swanne-hooke or crook. Stealing cygnets which had flown out of bounds, taking eggs from a nest, building a weir on a river where swans fed, and many other offenses carried heavy penalties. To ensure quiet nesting for the pampered birds between the feast of Easter and the "Sunday next after Trinity," no duck hunting was allowed and "no snares or nettes for ye taking of Bitternes" were permitted. The bittern is now so rare in Britain that it is under special protection.

During the reign of Henry VIII the lands around the old village of Abbotsbury fell to Sir Giles Strangeways, ancestor of the Earl of Illchester. When Elizabeth I ascended the throne these lands had been inherited by a widow, Joan Strangeways. Lady Joan and her steward had not yet marked the new cygnets or even the adult birds which had flown in to nest, when the Queen, accompanied by a considerable suite, arrived unexpectedly on a visit. The entire establishment was occupied in accommodating the guests and, in the flurry, no thought was given to the seasonal swan-marking. Elizabeth, at the time of her departure, ordered her servants to collect all the unmarked swans and the cygnets as well, for shipment to her already overflowing swanneries. The transporting of five hundred intractable birds must have been

a considerable operation in those days (according to a record dated 1282, seven men and seven horses were hired to convey a mere fourteen swans from the herd of the Bishop of Winchester to Taunton Manor in Somerset). Of course the Queen was acting within her rights and no one dared question her.

All swans owned by private individuals were required to be marked on the bill with a puncturing device, and during the sixteenth century there were said to be 900 brands in use. The only exception were the swans of Abbotsbury which are to this day marked with a single nick on the web of the foot. A swan-mark, called *ciginota*, was a possession of considerable value and was personal to the owner who could, however, sell it at will. In many cases marked birds belonged to an estate and were part of an inheritance.

Even today a swan not marked is the property of the Crown. It must be a painful ordeal for the cygnet to have the royal mark—no less than five crowns—incised on its tender pinkish mandible.

Oxford University has its game of swans on the River Isis and uses its old-time mark, a cross with arms of equal length. Cambridge also has its fluctuating games and flights, its mark being three buckles. Swans are kept on a small ornamental water in the ancient enclosure of Emmanuel

College in Cambridge, and sometimes are seen flying above the buildings of the old University town.

Aside from royalty, the most distinguished swan-holders in London at the present time are the ancient guilds. The Vintners Company, perhaps the oldest surviving city guild, and the Dyers own all the swans on the Thames from Blackfriars Bridge to Henley, thirty miles or more away. A recent census sets the number of swans at fifteen hundred, an increase of around seven hundred since the end of World War II. Early each August the celebrated swan-upping (originally swan-round-upping) takes place, when members of both companies gather their spring-hatched cygnets and mark them on the bill.

Formerly this swan-upping was a colorful pageant, for the participants wore brilliant liveries: the Dyers blue, the Vintners blue and white, the royal swan-master and his assistants bright scarlet. In the procession up the river the barges were propelled by uniformed oarsmen. Now it is a less entertaining occasion but still impressive, organized from the Lord Chamberlain's office and extending over a week. While the royal swan-master, or Keeper of the Queen's Swans, still participates, the swan-uppers now carry out their work in skiffs and wearing conventional slacks and jerseys. However, the markers themselves are distinguished by blazers: Dyers in plain bright blue, Vintners in striped blue and white.

Catching a reluctant swan is an art not easily acquired. A few of the "uppers" wield crooks to catch the bird by the neck. Then a man grasps the neck of the cygnet with one hand, while with the other hand he folds back the two feet over the wings. This must be done with great care and skill, for a blow from the wing of even a half-grown cygnet carries terrific impact and can easily break a man's arm.

The ancient marks are still used. The Dyers' is a simple

notch on the side of the bill, the Vintners' a double chevron. The sign of The Swan with Two Necks sometimes seen hanging over an old-time inn is a corruption of The Swan with Two Nicks.

These guilds of London indulge in an annual swan feast during which birds of suitable age are roasted with appropriate sauces and ceremonies. The guilds also provide swans for the sumptuous banquets given by the Lord Mayor. A birth certificate is almost a necessity in choosing a swan for the table, for the meat is exceedingly tough if the bird is over three years old, and a swan can retain a deceptively sleek appearance up to sixty, seventy, even eighty years of age. A full-grown cygnet, two or three years old, in its first white plumage with just a feather or two of gray, is considered the most palatable.

Recently a hotel in Queen's Gate, Kensington, opened an Elizabethan restaurant where swan is on the menu. But it took a long time before the serving of the royal bird in a restaurant could be carried out. The difficulty lay in procuring swans. There is, however, a curious survival of the old swan-eating custom in the County of Norfolk. There a swan-pit is owned by St. Helen's Hospital, one of the oldest, most beautiful and, at the same time, least known of the English medieval foundations for the aged. The building stands in Bishopsgate Street in the town of Norwich and houses a hundred and fifty old people. In olden times the swan-pit was maintained to provide an annual feast for the inmates. Swans may now be purchased there. Cygnets from the neighboring rivers are impounded early in August, under special license, and are fed cut grass and barley until they weigh around fifteen pounds, when they are considered fit for the table. The swan-pit, constructed of brick, is seventy feet long by thirty-four feet wide and is filled to a depth of two feet by constantly running water where the birds rest and preen.

The multiplication of swans may eventually place the royal bird on the list of game birds. In many places on the island of Britain the swan population has actually doubled, with the consequence that naturalists and conservationists alike are considering control. Swans are big birds and naturally aggressive. They are already encroaching on the limited quarters of valuable game birds by interfering with their nesting and by consuming the available water weeds. In some places they have actually driven away rare species which were being encouraged to breed again after long absences.

In 1954 and 1955 a painstaking census of Mute swans in the United Kingdom was launched in Scotland, supported by the British Trust for Ornithology in Oxford. The object was to ascertain the number of breeding swans and the size of nonbreeders in Scotland, England, and Wales. The help of the public was enlisted in the tremendous task of swan counting.

The response was gratifying though a bit bewildering, for as many as thirty individuals reported the same roadside nests. However, the final estimate covered areas seldom visited by professional bird watchers, and it was prodigious for the small area studied: over 18,000 swans and 3,650 occupied nests. Most of the nesting birds were counted in the southeast, Dorset winning, with County Kent a runner-up; Wales and Scotland lagged far behind. This census was an attempt to count only the native Mute swans, ignoring the wild Whoopers and Bewick's.

In England, as in parts of the United States, civilization is constantly encroaching on the habitat of the water birds. Fens and marshlands are being drained. Areas which not long ago were park land with ornamental lakes and quiet stretches of water are being put into cultivation and hemmed in by dwelling houses. Frequently village ponds are drained and planted. Yet each year there are more and more swans and, consequently, more and more cygnets, all requiring water room.

It is feared that an open season on swans may be the only solution. Great wisdom must be exercised in dealing with the problem, for the English are a conservative people, not likely to sit down to a Sunday dinner of royal swan instead of the traditional roast beef and Yorkshire pudding. The swan has been for so long a privileged personality and a part of their daily life that the very idea of its long beautiful neck upon the executioner's block may well be repugnant to them.

Every small English town or village seems to have its own swan story, and all evince a pride in swans. These birds inspire personal affection in the people who live with them and know them. The swans of the Cathedral city of Wells,

with their families, have occupied the moat surrounding the ancient palace of the bishop for as long as anyone can remember. In the gatehouse over the water there is a small window from which dangles a string attached to a bell. When the swans feel they need something to eat they pull the string and tinkle the bell, and bread is always thrown out for them. The little ducks who share the moat watch enviously for they cannot pull the bell.

Then there is Godfrey, "the injured swan of the Isle of Man," an established character whose portrait appears on Christmas cards designed to raised funds for the local branch of the S.P.C.A.

Godfrey is a wild Mute who lived, mateless, on a clear pond that had formed in a disused quarry. A storm threw him against the cliff, breaking his wing. The kindly police of the island took him to Sir Douglas Young, who has a lake on his estate of Ballasalla near Castletown. Here Godfrey lived contentedly with the ducks and the coots, until one day a longing to visit his old quarry seized him. He was seen walking down the paved highway into the town. It was a long journey and he became discouraged with his inability to fly, for he waddled into the Castletown railway station and placed himself in the ticket queue.

The station master telephoned Lady Young, "Milady, your swan is standing in the ticket queue waiting to buy a ticket. What shall I do?"

Milady drove down to the station and taxied Godfrey out to his quarry where he swam around for a while. Then, satisfied, he returned to his sequestered lake. Godfrey now has a mate, another wounded Mute found dying on a mud bank at Ramsey in the north of the island. Gilbert is of uncertain sex also, but a nest has been built. The question now is, "Which swan will lay the eggs?"

The Royal Birds

Johnny, also of the Isle of Man, is another swan character. He has been lording it over the small seaport of Peel for as long as the oldest old-timer can remember. No one knows Johnny's age. He is big even for a Mute, and he wears a ribbon around his neck with a tinkling bell attached. When tourists crowd the little town in summer, he keeps busy showing them around. He leads them to the castle, shows them the harbor, and the many sights of this old-world resort. He takes them into the shops and into the houses as well. He is said to take every occasion to go where kippers are smoked, when his appetite sharpens. He is somewhat of a nuisance, and at one time a few citizens started a petition to have him removed so that he could not promenade on the main thoroughfare so frequently. But the idea proved very unpopular, and Johnny remains at large.

Recently there was an extraordinary instance of sea gulls feeding a swan trapped in an icebound pond in Scotland. The unfortunate bird, frozen into the ice, was kept alive by his natural enemies until the thaw. It is very unusual for swans to allow themselves to be trapped in ice. When severe cold overtakes them on a pond or a lake they keep an open space around the herd by continually swimming and circling to break up the formation of ice. This swan, though, seems to have been alone and was probably unable to keep awake.

Swans do have their natural enemies, and one of these is, surprisingly, the loon. The most primitive of all birds, the fossil remains of his ancestors being almost identical with his present form, the loon is considered the lowest of the low. But he knows how to take care of himself and how to defend his nesting rights. He waits and watches for an opportunity to destroy the big swan's eggs with sharp taps of his formidable bill.

Loons, along with otters, foxes, eagles, ravens—even crows and large gulls—may help in the reduction of a too large swan population. But swans are wise birds, and may settle the problem themselves as the Black swan has done in Australia. There, during prolonged droughts, the Black swan either reduces the number of eggs laid or altogether refrains from nesting until conditions improve.

England is not the only country with a swan problem; Denmark too has its troubles. The Mute was not given full protection in that small kingdom until 1925, when it was estimated that there were only two or three pairs of wild Mutes in the whole country. However, a recent census by K. Paludan and J. Fog reveals that there are now upward of 728 breeding pairs and several thousands of nonbreeding swans. This total in Denmark does not include domesticated swans in parks or on private estates.

The sight of a pair of swans gliding on a lake or flying low across the loops of a river is strangely exciting. At the sound of the great wings tearing the air close above their heads, townspeople pause and look up to catch a momentary glimpse of romance in their everyday humdrum lives.

I remember a certain rain-threatening night in Cambridge when the Midsummer Fair was in full swing. Five serenely regal swans, incandescent in the glare from the carrousel lights, came swimming silently along the black slow-flowing surface of the Cam River. Looking neither to the right nor to the left, ignoring the tinsel and the noise, slender necks erect, powerful webs churning long lines of rainbowed ripples, they surged toward some peaceful resting place. These protégés of royalty, wild no longer, live in a world of their own, a world far removed from our frenzied civilization.

ॐ 2 ॐ

The Mutes

THE MOST FAMILIAR swan in the world is the Mute, *Cygnus olor,* the semiwild swan of the British Isles and northern Europe. This is perhaps the most beautiful of the whole race, and you know it as it swims with curved neck and stiffly arched pinions on the dark waters of our ornamental lakes. There is surely no bird more conscious of its own beauty. It is no wonder the ancient Greeks saw in it the embodiment of their goddess Aphrodite, the symbol of love, and of Apollo, the god of poetry and of the sun.

The Mutes

Mutes are so easy to domesticate that many believe them to be a completely tame species. They seem naturally disposed to association with Man and are content to nest and raise their families in one small area instead of migrating long distances in the fall and in the spring.

The Mute is one of the largest of the swan family, approximating and sometimes even exceeding the great Trumpeter of North America in size and wing span. A big cob may be four and a half feet tall with wings spreading nine or even ten feet. It is easy to recognize, for its bill is bright orange with a base and prominent knob or "berry" of jet black. The large webbed feet are black and exceedingly strong.

These Mutes are considered bad-tempered and even dangerous by those who know them only in the confined water of public parks. There crowds of unthinking visitors constantly irritate them and feed them bread, which is an unnatural food for them. Fierce they certainly are, but not without cause. An angry Mute cob has been known to crush a heavy galvanized bucket with one stroke of his wing, but the aggressor was removing his precious cygnets in order to brand them, and the swan's rage was justified. However, they are quiet and even friendly when they are not abused.

The Mute is not really as voiceless as his name implies, though compared to the Whooper he is silent, particularly in flight. In captivity Mutes growl, hiss, bark, and even trill. Occasionally they utter a loud and startling trumpet cry, a warning of danger to the herd.

In England and parts of the European continent these swans are resident the year round and can be watched at close quarters. In England in particular they nest and raise their families, not only on the ancient sanctuaries such as Abbotsbury and Claremont, but on quiet lakes and rivers and even beside the village pond or a slow-moving streamlet bordering the highway. From the top of a double-decker bus I have looked right down into a Mute swan's nest and have seen the parents handing out first principles of education to a bevy of fluffy cygnets.

Mute swans in England seem to realize that they are protected by royal decree, and because the climate is never too severe, they need not fly long distances to breed and nest. It is true they do not always remain in the same place. Even the swans of Abbotsbury leave the somewhat exposed waters of the Fleet in wintertime to pass a few months in a warmer locality. However, they do not go far and they always come back to their original nest and to their former friends, unless some danger makes this inadvisable.

A Mute is a creature of habit, but even at Abbotsbury, where a check has been kept on its movements for over a thousand years, there have been fluctuations in numbers. In the summer of 1880 the number of swans there reached the all-time high of fifteen hundred. The following winter the weed *zostera marina*, commonly called eelgrass, was frozen into the ice by the excessive cold (remembered to this day as The Great Frost) and was torn out by the roots and swept away by exceptionally high spring tides. This marine growth, which looks like a coarse grass, is the mainstay of a swan's diet. Therefore, despite supplementary feeding, a number of the birds died while others simply flew away, reducing the number to a bare four hundred. That year there was only one nest. In 1932 a fungus growth killed the weed not only on the eastern but on the western shores of the Atlantic, and once more the number of resident swans dwindled, for they never thrive on artificial feeding.

Abbotsbury is an ideal place to observe the home life of the Mute swan. It is a time-honored village of old stone houses with a huge fourteenth-century thatched barn and

Zostera Marina

the remains of an abbey founded in the eleventh century by
Edward the Confessor. The Fleet itself is a narrow lagoon
seven miles long, bordered by lush reed beds and protected
from the waters of the English Channel by the high bank

of celebrated Chesil Beach. The beautiful old town of Dorchester is only a few miles away, and Weymouth Bay can be seen from the heights above Abbotsbury. The water is slightly brackish, but a rivulet called the Drinking Stream feeds it at the western end, and the natural food supply is plentiful. The swans, owned by Lord Illchester, come and go as they please and are entirely self-supporting. Swanherds are always on duty to protect and care for them, the chief swanherd, Fred Lexter, being the fourth in succession of his family to hold the honored post.

During the winter many of the swans depart, taking their young cygnets with them. But in the early spring they return and, from the end of April to late in September, the swannery is open to visitors. The sight of so many swans is breath-taking. There are usually about 800, walking, nesting, preening, swimming. Great flights come sailing in, churning up the water as they brake their speed with a forward thrust of their great feet. Filmy feathers, the ultimate in whiteness, float around for you to retrieve and carry home as mementos. Fuzzy cygnets can be seen, penned away from interference,

it is true, but regarding you with the bright and interested eyes of adolescence.

Visitors are not admitted during the mating time, for then the swans are often dangerous and unpredictable. Many years ago, though, a beautiful and slender lady with lustrous eyes was allowed to enter the gates day after day to watch the performance. She was the greatest of all dancers, the incomparable Anna Pavlova. In the ballet "The Swan" she danced her impressions to the music of Saint-Saëns for audiences throughout the world.

A swan mates for life, and if the bird of its choice dies or is killed it rarely remates, though it may live to the Biblical three score years and ten. This explains why a beautiful mature cob or pen attaches itself to a family group. It is, in most cases, a widow or widower and as such is acceptable as baby sitter or mother's helper. It shows affection for the foster cygnets and takes care of a series of families through the years.

Unlike the human race, swans never seem to age. They remain, cob and pen, sparklingly white, agile, strong, and beautiful. Perennially serene and lovely, they celebrate the return of spring and mating time. Here is no male strutting for an apparently indifferent female, no avid female chasing a reluctant male. Both are uplifted and uninhibited, curving and stretching their long necks, rising on the tips of their ebony feet, leaping and pirouetting like ballerinas. After forty years of marriage, when two hundred or more offspring have been raised, educated, and sent out into the world, the parent swans still dance for the very joy of living.

Swans are not shy; they care nothing for people, and if you have the luck to be at the right spot at the right time you can see performed this Swan Lake ballet. Swans all over the world have some routine nuptial dance, but that of the Mute is surely one of the loveliest.

It is popularly supposed that a swan does not build a nest. This is not true. Nest-building is a serious business and is one of the lessons a cygnet is painstakingly taught. At first sight, the structure looks like a shaggy mound, but in fact it is scientifically designed. It is built upon a firm but

porous base, which allows water to drain through without damaging it. It is so cleverly constructed that it will actually float over the troubled waters like a miniature Noah's Ark. If you could climb up and sit on it you would find it as soft and springy as your own armchair.

If not driven away from the selected spot, the same pair will return year after year to re-line and remodel the structure and clear up the debris of winter. This remodeling is continued all through the incubation period, the sitting bird occupying its leisure in picking up sticks within reach of its long neck and fitting the pieces around herself wherever needed. Thus the nest of an older pair may measure as much as six feet across and two or three feet in height.

Even a minor flood does not discourage these birds. Eggs which have been under water for two or three days have been known to hatch out normally if steadily incubated as soon as the water has receded. Eggs vary greatly in number, but six cygnets seem to make the average family among the wilder, unsupervised Mute swans. In sanctuaries nine young are usual, while families of twelve have been recorded.

The eggs are a long oval in shape and bluish green in color, quite unlike the cream or white eggs of other northern swans. Incubation is a wearisome thirty-five to forty days. It is shared by both sexes, the cob taking the more perilous night watch and the pen sitting by day.

The ceremony of changing the guard is fascinating to watch. I have seen it many times. The pen walks quietly up to the nest and touches the sleepy cob on the head. He rouses himself. Then they rub bills, twine necks, and preen each other's feathers with all signs of affection. At last the cob raises himself and, balanced by half-spread wings, turns the eggs carefully, using bill and feet dexterously. Now the pen climbs up beside him, and together they seem to admire

their handiwork. She picks up a fallen twig, he leans over
to retrieve another, and they proceed to tidy the nest. Then
the cob rises and steps down, and the pen moves forward
with raised wings and lowers herself, breast first, onto her
treasure. She shuffles a little this way and that, her long
neck curving gracefully until, with one last look, her mate
moves away. Then she settles down with her neck laid along
her back and her bill buried in a fluff of feathers.

When the long vigil is over and the eggs start cracking,
the cob, dismayed and bewildered like any human father,
takes himself off. But the pen knows just what to do. She
casts out the eggshells, tidies the nursery, and fluffs out her
feathers to protect and dry the little nestlings.

Soon they emerge, beautiful little puffs of pearl gray,
with necks a trifle longer than goslings, neat little profiles,
black bills and feet, and astonishingly bright black eyes. They
toddle around the nest but do not eat or go near the water
until the second or third day, when they are able to paddle
about. Later they are taught to swim.

The Mutes

Most of the English cygnets belonging to the Crown and to private owners and companies are marked in August, when they are about four months old. But the babies of Abbotsbury are marked on the first or second day, depending on the hour of hatching. Each baby has the web of his little foot punctured with a single nick, and, though he may leave the Fleet and travel far, as many of them do, he will always bear the proud insigne of his birthplace. Marking does not seem to hurt them much. They chirp a little and their indignant parents bark and growl, but after the ordeal cob and pen sort out their youngsters and lead them back to the nest area where they belong.

Later in the year when visitors (42,157 by actual count in one short season) flock down to this sanctuary, the cygnets are penned in large wire enclosures, twenty to thirty in a cage, each attended by an adult swan who is probably widowed. There seems to be no quarreling or resentment on the part of the parents or their cygnets. When at last the visitors depart at 4:30 o'clock and the kindergarten is released, the

offspring are sorted out amicably and each family waddles off to its sleeping quarters, usually the original nest.

These nests at Abbotsbury are placed close together, as little as four or five yards apart, and each family guards its territory as in the wild, raising wings to threaten anyone who ventures near. They hiss and growl and even bark like small dogs if their cygnets are approached. Foxes, otters, weasels, ravens, even large gulls and crows are a menace to young cygnets. Sometimes at night a sitting cob gives voice to a loud trumpeting, a haunting cry ending with a tremulous vibration. The sound is comparable to the call of the red deer and is an alert to warn the whole swan community of danger.

Mutes are so accustomed to protection that they nest in open places exposed to the view of even the most casual passer-by. The female sits high like a queen on her nest, and the male sometimes sits beside her, picking up twig after twig and passing it to her while she stretches her long neck to receive it and deftly fits it around her to mould the structure to the shape of her body. No hiding in the tall weeds for her majesty the Mute.

The education of the cygnets is a major undertaking and continues for several months. Baby swans have to be trained meticulously to uphold their royal status. Both cob and pen, ruffled with pride, are their instructors.

The youngsters take it all with a mixture of seriousness and carefree delight. Their intelligent little eyes sparkle as they watch their mother's demonstration of up-ending. Of course she does not exactly up-end. To preserve her dignity as a swan, she lets her neck hang low at the waterline. It is very mobile so that she can reach the bottom without in-

dulging in the ungainly tip-up of the ducks. Cygnets, until they have attained their true swan necks, must tip the tail well up, and this they are painstakingly taught to do. They dutifully thrust their heads under the water and stick their wiggling tufts of tail skyward. At first only the head and part of the neck is submerged. They try again and, with a parental push, they reach the bottom from where a dripping green morsel can be dragged up and triumphantly displayed. But the watchful mother may take it from the little bill and flip it away, for some water weeds seem to be unsuitable. The cygnet has to learn that too.

Cygnets of course can swim from an early age. They paddle around and follow their parents in a compact little convoy. But exhibition swimming has to be learned. That sublime, seemingly effortless surge across the still water, that nonchalant breasting of a river in spate, that regal spurning of the rip-tide in an estuary, has to be learned.

The fall of a mill sluice is a good place to practice, so the little flock is led to the rush of water to paddle strenuously against the stream. It is exhausting. The small heads bob, the down-covered wings are assiduously raised and lowered, while the black webbed feet paddle and paddle and the cob and pen bend their graceful necks in encouragement.

At last, worn out but exultant, the young are permitted

to relax and float back with the current, while the smallest and weariest are invited to climb onto a parent's back to ride serenely home on a springy cushion of billowing white feathers.

When very small the cygnet is helped to its perch by the parent's spreading a wing low over the water, making an inclined runway to safety. Later, the parent merely sinks into the water low enough for the small one to climb aboard. Sometimes the baby for some reason does not want to ride and will deliberately fall off again and again, while the mother growls and barks like a sea lion.

As soon as the cygnets are half grown, another lesson must be learned: nest building. This is amusing and not as strenuous as the swimming lesson. The youngsters, led ashore, group themselves around their parents to observe them as they pull down bullrushes and reeds to weave them together in the traditional form. Sometimes the lesson occupies a full hour, the structure being torn apart again and again so that some particular point can be stressed. Then the practice nest is abandoned to a coot or a moorhen, who likes to use several nests at a time.

Much later the cygnets must be taught to fly. The young have no strong flight feathers until after the autumn molt, though their funny little bare wings are sometimes raised like downy stumps, in imitation of their parents' glorious white pinions. However, just as the leaves are turning color and the air grows sharp and winelike, the dismal molting is over and they have wings. Wings! There can be nothing in human experience to parallel this ecstatic moment of release from the mud and the reedy water to the clear infinity of the air!

A full-grown Mute's wingspread may measure as much as nine feet, for he is the heaviest bird that flies, and the cygnet is now three-quarters grown, though not mature. The huge muscles that carry his parents so swiftly and effortlessly are not fully developed, yet he has eight or even ten pounds' weight to lift into the air. Therefore first attempts to fly lead to ignominious nose-dives. But soon the youngster is airborne and away, skimming unsteadily along, with pen or cob, devoted as ever, in close attendance. The novice at first flies only a few feet above its parent so that it can safely drop onto the strong back at intervals. It will fly only fifty or sixty feet and land lightly on the safe "carrier" below, until it can rise again of its own accord and try once more. Eventually it will attain a speed of one hundred miles per hour.

Young birds dive and swim under water, but later they seem unable or reluctant to submerge completely. The adult can sink his whole body low into the water or raise it high with uplifted pionions—busking as it is called in Old English —like a ship sailing with spinnakers set.

It is hard to realize the power and speed of a swan on the water. His great webbed feet carry him along without

apparent effort even against the swirl of the tide, and when a thirty-five-pound cob is angry and gives chase, beware! He raises his mighty wings, lowers his chest, curves his neck forward and down. Churning up the water before him, he rushes forward in an incredible spurt, propelling himself in sinister jerks by moving both feet at once. Even on land swans can travel fast when necessary, though their usual walk is ungainly owing to the habit of folding the foot and lifting it high with each step.

In spite of their intensive training these semitame birds do not seem able to learn to estimate the lethal menace of modern motor-driven traffic. They often nest close to heavily traveled highways, and there are many casualties. Sometimes an incubating pen is killed trying to beat a high-powered Jaguar across the road. Then the unhappy and bewildered cob must take over the entire business of hatching, raising, and educating the family. He usually makes an expert job of it, but the following year he resigns himself to the role of widower. It is unlikely that he will remate, though he may live for many more years.

Accidents of this kind occur in London where the river swans, instead of swimming under the arches, persist in flying over the bridges thronged with swift-moving traffic. Even on a clear day it takes an alert driver to avoid the flight over the parapet. In the fog it is impossible.

One day when I was riding in a bus on Westminster Bridge, a swan loomed up suddenly, a white apparition, and the impact was tremendous. The lovely eight-foot wings flailed at the closed windows till the body fell crumpled among the wildly swerving cars. As the frantic spouse zoomed over the rail to land beside his stricken mate, a policeman's shrill whistle halted the stream of traffic. The passers-by waited, some with actual tears in their eyes, while the driver of the bus held the now docile cob until an ambulance from the nearest R.S.P.C.A. station arrived.

A swan is almost sacred in England. To see it crumpled and bleeding, its long, graceful neck laid low in the mud, its plumage spattered, is to see tragedy. In other matters swans show intelligence, but in all the years they seem not to have learned to go under instead of over the Thames bridges.

These Thames swans move around very little. But in many localities the first nip of cold in the air makes them restless and, accompanied by their adolescent offspring, they fly off to winter on some sheltered creek or river not far away.

Swans marked in England have been recognized in Holland and Denmark, but the population in most places has remained more or less stable until lately. During World War II Abbotsbury, being within easy distance of the Naval Base at Weymouth, was almost deserted by the birds on account of the bombing. But as soon as things quieted down they came back, and improved conditions have resulted in maintaining a slight increase over their former number. The swans here seem to match their numbers to local conditions, for they rarely exceed a thousand. Elsewhere, particularly in Dorset and Kent, this is not the case.

Casualties among wild birds were rare during World War II. Down to the smallest sparrow they all seemed to possess an inherent instinct when a bombing was imminent. Long before Man's radar could pick up the warning of approaching planes, the birds flew off, to return unruffled when the raid was over. During the worst of the battle over London a biologist requested dead starlings for research, but no dead starlings were found, though starlings throng the heart of the city in such numbers as to be rated a nuisance. There is, however, one recorded instance of a London sparrow who fainted in Kensington Gardens during a raid.

Swans are undoubtedly equipped with this supersensitive warning device, for war casualties noted were extremely low. Their numbers were certainly not seriously diminished, as the recent phenomenal increase shows. War is for Man, not these wild ones who have their own independent life path.

❧ 3 ❧

Whoopers in Winter

THE GREAT WHOOPER, monarch of the airways of Northern Europe, is a truly wild swan. This magnificent bird is one of the largest of all wild swans, equaled in size only by the Trumpeter of North America. It measures over sixty inches from bill tip to tail tip and has a wingspread of from eight to nine feet.

The cry of these birds, as they sweep by, echoes and re-echoes: whoo-ha—whoo-ha—whoo-ha—the double note given three times with the second syllable at a higher pitch than the first. But when they settle on water they come in quietly one after another, like transatlantic planes, and start to swim with heads held high and broad backs sleek and smooth. They disdain to curve their necks and busk their wings as the Mutes do, for their nobility is self-evident.

The Whooper so resembles the Trumpeter of North America that it was once thought to be merely a variation of the same species. However, the color of the bill readily distinguishes it from its western counterpart. It shows a large area of bright chrome yellow bordered and tipped with black, whereas the Trumpeter's bill is uniformly black.

Stories of Whooper swans are rare, for the Whooper is wild and wary of men. There is, however, a tale of St. Hugh of Lincoln in which such a swan is definitely described. St. Hugh, the beloved bishop of Lincoln, who lived at the end of the twelfth century, had a gift for taming wild birds. It is recorded that at his enthronement a wild swan "such as never had before been seen" flew over his head to shield him from the sun, and henceforth attached itself to his person, fed from his hand, and stood guard over him when he walked abroad. Friendship of animals for saints is not uncommon in these old stories, but this was no ordinary swan. It is described as being "white and exceeding large, but unlike the usual bird in that he did not exhibit the knob and black color on the bill but had, in truth, the bill flat and adorned with yellow." Obviously a Whooper swan.

The whooper is a noisy bird, not only on the wing but on the water as well. The voice of the cob is loud and penetrating, while that of the pen is, as it should be, mellow and pleasing. At times a wintering pair will call to each other in a musical duet, necks pumping up and down and wings shaking in a temperamental operatic aria. They have many notes. Sometimes they indulge in a prolonged twittering and trilling, with a long rolling effect. The male has a low musical song of his own, seven distinct notes rising slightly, then falling, then rising again. Indeed, this swan was once called *Cygnus musica,* and the French still cling to the name *Cygne chantant* (singing swan), while the Germans call it *Sing-schwan.* It is now listed officially as *Cygnus-cygnus-cygnus,* which perhaps means superswan.

The Whooper probably inspired the legend of the dying-swan song. One authority prosaically surmises that the story is based on the fact that any bird shot and wounded at a height might exhale the air from its windpipe as it descends, producing a flute-like sound. In the case of a swan, the windpipe is extra long and circumvoluted, so that such a sound would be prolonged and clear. This is the ornithologist's sternly scientific view.

H. W. Robinson, the naturalist, in writing of a mortally wounded swan shot while flying high, says:

> Wings fixed, he commenced at once his song which was continued until the water was reached nearly a mile away. Never before or since have I heard anything like the song of this stricken swan. It sounded at times like the running notes of an octave, most plaintive in character and musical in tone and, as the sound was borne to us, mellowed by the distance, we stood astounded and could only exclaim, "We have heard the song of a dying swan."

Certainly neither he nor his companion ever willingly shot a swan again.

Whoopers do not travel as far in search of a nesting place as do the intrepid, miniature Bewick's swans. Some of them have been observed to breed and raise their young in the Highlands of Scotland, although Iceland and Lapland are the favored localities. Little is known of the European

wild swans in their northern nesting places, but wild swans all over the world have much the same habits. The Whoopers observed in Scotland built the usual large structure with materials found nearby. One nest in the Highlands, which contained four yellowish-white eggs, was described as being near an island where herons congregated, in a patch of grass, blueberries, and heather.

James Fisher, the celebrated English naturalist, has given me permission to quote his description of swans in Iceland:

> Whoopers in Iceland in June are seen flying white against the black bastions of Thjorsa's Gorge, the big River of the Bull where the pink-footed ganders stand guard by their sitting geese. In July, the swans disappear out of the skyscape of the tundra, for they are flightless then in their long molt. Then you hear them whooping. If you are tired with the long day's watch, they sound like donkeys braying for their mothers. But another day they may bring you from your sleeping tent as trumpeters of morning with their music of clanging, their magic music of bells.

He goes on to say:

> There's a lake in central Iceland called Hvitarvatn, the White Water, and from each side of a little mountain a glacier tumbles into it from the icecap of Langjokull. Now and then in summer little icebergs break away and float across the lake. On the opposite side a stream flows into the lake through a green willow-meadow, all covered with saxifrage and Dryas and cotton grass and Grass of Parnassus, where the Whoopers have their brown nest mounds of dead water-weeds and grass. Some days the lake is blue, some days grey, some days nearly black. . . . The icebergs and the swans are white, floating together like the molted feathers of the mother of all swans.

Geoffrey Grigson, who accompanied the scientist, described the Whoopers in this poetic passage:

I've seen them in Iceland too, swans in pairs . . . winging down the almost terrifying perspective of those wide and low, desolate and bare Icelandic river valleys, so white, the only living things in the endless view. That is when you believe in the swan tales . . . the swans that are humans changed to birds. . . . In Iceland I have almost felt I might turn a corner by the edge of one of the pools and see a swan-maiden with her coat of swan feathers laid by her on the cold, black basalt.

These passages refer to the Whoopers in their northern nesting territory, cold and remote and inaccessible to the majority of their admirers. There is little information about the life of these swans in summertime, though a French naturalist who observed them in Lapland speaks of the pen sitting exposed on her lofty nest like a snowcap on a miniature mountain, while the devoted male crouched below, his long neck stretched up and his brilliant bill laid beside hers as she incubated her eggs.

The pen apparently builds the nest herself while the male collects and passes the materials to her. Eggs are a creamy white, readily nest-soiled, and they average only four or five. They are laid on alternate days, and usually hatch at the same time.

Even this small number of eggs does not explain the

dearth of young cygnets accompanying their parents on their first migration. All young swanlets are the prey of predators by land and air and water, no matter where they are hatched and raised, but the case of the Whooper babies seems particularly tragic.

In the western section of Iceland, in Northern Lapland, and along the coasts where the birds nest, there is a tremendous eagle, far larger than the familiar Golden eagle, called the White-tailed Erne (*Haliaetus albicilla*). This enormous buteo measures forty-one inches from bill to tail, with a tremendous wing span and cruelly strong taloned feet. He is able to attack and overcome a weakling roe deer and is the inveterate enemy of the swans. This predator no doubt is responsible for the loss of many cygnets even before they start on their perilous journey south.

Migration must be a severe ordeal for the young Whoopers. They fly lower than most swans even on sustained journeys, and almost the entire flight south from Iceland lies

over the stormy waters of the North Atlantic. One survivor out of a clutch of four or five indicates a terrible rate of mortality.

These wildest of wild swans prefer lakes in a mountainous setting, with good reed beds and shallows suitable for feeding. Where the water is a trifle deep even the adults up-end, and where it is stained with iron oxide or mud their beautiful supple necks become tinged with color. The waters of the Cumberland Lakes, however, are singularly clear and limpid, and there the birds remain pristinely white.

Their favorite haunt is Elterwater, that jewel ringed with bluebell woods which lies beneath the rugged Langdale Pikes. This is the first lake they come to when they fly in from the North, and it is interesting to learn that the name Elterwater is derived from the old Norse *Elptarvatn*, which means swan lake. This obscure mountain refuge must long have been the stopping place of the Whoopers.

Whoopers in winter quarters delight in greeting each flight of newcomers with loud trumpeting and wing-waving, while the arrivals, in their turn, reply with a tumult of loud cries. As each new group flies in, every bird, down to the smallest shrill-voiced cygnet, sounds his horn—bass, treble, or alto—and, as they alight, they are greeted with an answering chorus and loud wing-flapping.

This display of greeting in birds of such size is particularly unusual because there is nothing belligerent about it. The newcomers are being welcomed by those already in possession, and the procedure does not vary. The original group approaches the weary travelers, and the leading bird raises and lowers his head, trumpeting on a pleasing two-tone note. Then the others join in a chorus—whoo-ha—whoo-ha—like a muted town band.

Even a short flight around the lake, if only for exercise, is accompanied by cries of whoo-ha—whoo-ha. Often, while quietly feeding, one of the big cobs will be inspired to turn away from the crowd to face a purely imaginary interloper. Then he will trumpet and move his head up and down, while the other birds feed quietly and take no notice of him.

Sometimes just before the spring flight back to the North, the mated couples practice their nuptial dance. Two birds, one as white and beautiful as the other, the pen a trifle smaller but otherwise indistinguishable, will face each other and rise in the water, breast to breast, with great wings waving and necks stretched high to greet each other with exultant cries. It is only a moment of ecstasy, a mere taste of the great day to come, for they go calmly back to their feeding or settle quietly down to sleep.

Swans rest with long necks laid along the back, head tucked in among the feathers. When they feel safe and sure, they close their eyes and really sleep. But if you are near, even if you think you are hidden from them, a bright black

eye is open and aware. They indulge in "pretense sleeping," for they are far too wary to allow you to catch them in an unguarded moment.

Siesta usually follows feeding in the early afternoon. Then the birds can be seen, floating well toward the center of the lake. Often one black foot is caught up on one side and the head is completely buried, but only if another bird happens to be on watch. Geese sometimes act as watchmen for a herd of swans if it is a herd that has been on friendly terms with them.

Any loud noise, and particularly any sudden noise, such as dogs barking, distant shots, shouting people, puts swans on the alert. A passing car does not worry them, but a car that stops, especially if it stops abruptly and the occupants get out, will send the whole herd into the air at once, the still waters of the lake churning under their running feet until they are up and away with a loud musical whoo-ha—whoo-ha.

In times of severe frost they will, with one accord, leave the higher altitudes and fly down to Windermere, the largest of the English lakes, where there is always open water even in the coldest weather. Here they unite in one huge herd and make an astonishing sight. Even though they are not as graceful and consciously ornamental as the well-known Mutes, there is a grandeur about them, particularly when they are grouped together in large numbers. The cygnets are only slightly smaller than their parents, dark gray with a clear white rim around the eye, which gives them an air of inquiring innocence. On a dull winter's day the chrome yellow on the bill of the adults is a striking color note as well as a sure identification. It is a clear primary color with no tinge of orange.

The herds remain in the lower altitude until the first hint of a thaw, accepting grain if the frost is really hard but disdaining bread. As soon as possible, however, they take off again to seek the lonely tarns and mountain lakes as far as possible from the haunts of Man.

At one time there were many Whooper swans in Greenland, nesting in the wilderness of bog and tundra in the interior. Toward the end of the last century, however, they were exterminated by the natives, who pursued and killed both adults and young birds during their molting period when they were unable to fly. Natives of the Arctic Circle, living as they do in bleak, nonproductive areas, are obliged to rely on very few natural resources, and swans supply not only food but warm clothing as well.

On the ground swans are clumsy and undignified, though the Whooper walks more gracefully than the Mute, lifting its feet well and moving briskly. In a fight it can overcome the larger bird, for it attacks without preliminary posturing, holding the wings partly out from the body, the head very low.

On the wing the Whooper becomes a creature of romance. Its wing music is a silken swish not heard at a great distance. Its cry is surely the most exciting, the most haunting of all wild sounds: Whoo-ha—whoo-ha—whoo-ha, rising and falling, with the deep bass of the veteran cob, the mellow contralto of the pen, the shrill bugling of the jubilant cygnets glorying in their suddenly realized strength and power. Not

even the Trumpeter in the days of his freedom could compare with a flight of Whoopers in full cry. Some people declare they are noisy, but to some people a Beethoven symphony is noisy, while to others it is the music of the spheres. The cry of the Whoopers is the music of earth and sky and distant places, the music of lonely lands and ice floes and blue water, the music of the aurora borealis.

Earth is so full of manmade noise that many people are

deaf to nature's harmonies. But, if you are lucky, you may wake one night to the cry of the wild swans overhead. Then you may sense, if only for a moment, the world of the ancients: centaurs and demigods of woodlands and rushing rivers.

❦ 4 ❧

In Europe and Asia

THE BEWICK'S SWAN was named for an English wood engraver who lived at Eltringham near Newcastle-on-Tyne in 1753. Not only was Thomas Bewick highly skilled in his art, but he worked with such love and understanding that his book on British birds, which appeared in 1797, proclaimed him a true naturalist as well. William Yarrel, an ornithologist of the period, refers to this in his *History of British Birds* published in 1843.

Among a considerable number [of swans] which had been forwarded to the London markets for sale, I was fortunate enough to select five examples of this new species. . . . I described it in a paper read before the Linnaean Society and proposed to call it Bewick's swan, thus devoting it to the memory of one whose beautiful and animated delineation of subjects in natural history entitles him to this tribute.

This account suggests that the Mute swan only was protected, and the visitors to the islands, the wild Whoopers and Bewick's, were killed and sold in large numbers.

Cygnus columbianus bewickii is the smallest of the northern swans, dainty, streamlined, intrepid, shy, and untamable. Northern swans are white, but the whiteness of the Bewick's seems to require an additional adjective to describe it. In the company of other swans, the frosty, almost incandescent quality of its plumage makes that of the other birds appear actually dingy.

This little swan nests as far north as possible, all along the fringes of the Arctic Sea, then east to the Lena River where a Russian swan, Jankowski, takes over. In winter the Bewick's can be seen in the British Isles, mostly along the coast, flying in long lines over the breaking waves. At times it ventures south into West Central Asia.

In England the Bewick's is not always recognized, though it often appears in large herds. It is, in fact, often mistaken for a large white goose. A gentle little swan with a pleasant voice, it would be most desirable as a permanent ornament in park lakes. However, more than any other of its kind it abhors mankind and civilization in general.

For years the Bewick's was considered merely an eastern variation of the North American Whistling Swan, but a closer study has placed it in its proper category. The bill of each shows a patch of yellow, but in the Whistler this color is confined to a very small area and is sometimes absent altogether, while on the bill of the Bewick's the bright chrome reaches beyond the nostrils.

Perhaps the greatest difference, however, is in the size and shape of the Bewick's, which is much smaller and distinctly gooselike. The head is chubby and round. The neck, definitely shorter, is always held meticulously erect. The legs and feet are black, and the flight is swift, but the wing-beat lacks the whistling wing-music of the American swan. Its voice in the air is a low-pitched, soft hoo-hoo-hoo, rather like the honking of a skein of geese. Moreover, except on long migrations, Bewick's is rarely seen flying in formation. Usually it flies in long straggling lines. On the ground it indulges in many conversational notes and, occasionally, before settling down to sleep in the evening, it gives voice to a faint, gentle crooning song, running the gamut of an octave in ascending and descending scale. The Bewick's can also bark sharply like a small dog and hiss in a most gooselike manner.

On lonely lakes and estuaries, particularly in Ireland, from Ulster right down to County Kerry, these pretty little

swans congregate in herds of several hundreds. You are indeed lucky if you come suddenly upon a sequestered lagoon where a vast flotilla of these dazzlingly white birds is assembled. They seem like beings from another sphere, and they take no notice of you unless you disturb them, for you belong to a different and quite negligible world in which they have no part.

One of the most favored resorts of these birds is Holland, particularly the new and artificially formed Isselmeer, that wide expanse of shallow water resulting from the damming of the Zuyder Zee. The original brine of this great sea-gulf has been gradually replaced by fresh water from the rivers which flow into the area, and here Bewick's swans assemble year after year in increasing numbers. They feed on the masses of *potamogetan*, a water weed that flourishes in shallow water and is much relished by swans. More and more Bewick's are flying into this swan paradise. From three to four thousand are counted there each winter and are affectionately named by the Hollanders *Kleine Zwann*.

They usually arrive in mid-October and remain only until late December. Then they all take wing and are seen no more until late in March, when they gather once again to prepare for their spring migration. It is not certain where they spend the interim, but it is possible that they fly over to the milder climate of Ireland, for Holland can be bitterly cold at the turn of the year.

In the far North where they spend the long light days of the Arctic summer, they nest on the remote islets that stud the estuaries of the gigantic rivers flowing out of Russia. They also frequent the marshy shallow lakes of that forsaken shoreline. Unlike most wild swans, they gather in colonies in that boundless expanse of wilderness, for the little Bewick's are gregarious, not only with their own kind but with other water birds as well.

Nests are conical in shape, smooth and symmetrical, built principally of clumps of moss intermixed with lichens, with an extra deep depression lined luxuriously with swan's-down. It is cold in those Arctic wastes even in summertime, although swans do not seem to feel the cold so long as they have sufficient food to warm their blood.

Laying begins in June; eggs number four, at most five, and incubation probably lasts as long as that of other better observed species. When the swanlets appear they are gray, with only the bills tipped with black and the feet a slaty gray. Both parents guard and train them, and conditions must be favorable, for there seems to be no shortage of first-year birds when they fly south. During the hazardous molting period there is apparently less human interference and fewer animal predators to reduce their numbers in the swamp-encircled wastelands which they have so wisely chosen as a nursery. Here under the midnight sun the Bewick's babies grow strong and learn to develop their wings. A safe and pleasant land—for swans.

By the time the young are ready to take part in the autumnal migration, their plumage is a dull grayish brown and the bill is clearly beginning to show its distinctive pattern.

The bright days shorten and darken, the ice begins to move into the estuaries, the shallow waters freeze over, and the water weeds on which they depend are completely locked away as if under glass. So southward they fly, spreading and fanning out, each group heading for its chosen wintering ground: some to England and Ireland; some to Holland, Denmark, and the Baltic; some down to the Black Sea and the Caspian; and some even as far as the Aral and West Central Asia.

The food they seek is mainly vegetable matter gleaned from the shallows, and the weeds they prefer are *Zostera marina, Zannichellia pedicellata, Potamogetan pectinatus,* all widely distributed not only in fresh but also in brackish water. Wild celery and the bulbous roots of aquatic plants as well as crustacea and water beetles are also on their menu. Swans do not and cannot eat fish, and stories of fish-destroying swans belong only to false rumor.

Family groups keep together throughout the winter and can easily be distinguished from the rest of the herd as they swim around some quiet lake among the larger numbers of nonbreeders. Bewick's are very hardy, young and old alike, but sometimes the exposed waters they have chosen become too bleak. During a prolonged and severe winter, they desert their usual territory and fly long distances to find a better shelter. In recent hard winters in Europe, they have flown into England in such large numbers that, in one case at least, food had to be dropped from helicopters where several hundreds were marooned on hard-frozen saltings. Food provided was usually grain with a quantity of bran and salvaged bread. Whole wheat bread was found acceptable, but white bread seems to have been considered by the swans fit only for humans.

Swans found in Norfolk may have flown in from their beloved haunt, the Isselmeer. This, being fresh water, freezes over quickly and hard, whereas the brackish estuaries and salt marshes of England's east coast remain open until the thermometer approaches zero.

Resembling the far-flying, cosmopolitan Bewick's is *Cygnus columbianus jankowski* from Russia. A distinct species, although similar to the Bewick's, this small Siberian swan leads an unsung and obscure existence behind an avian iron curtain where the Bewick's will not venture. Starting from the eastern bank of the Lena River, it nests along the desolate shores of the Siberian Sea as far as the Bering Strait which, for some inscrutable reason, it does not care to cross.

In wintertime it flies down into the little known plains and marshes of the eastern portion of Russia, penetrating into parts of China, particularly the upper waters of the Amur, the Yangtze, and the Hoang-ho, and even flying over to Japan and its adjacent islands. These swans are very numerous around Lake Baikal, where the nomad tribes and the Mongol horse and cattle breeders of the Buriat Republic have many tales to tell of them, some true, some legend. They are held in great respect. It is considered dangerous even to point a finger at this small number of the swan family. Therefore it is protected over most of its range, by means of this primitive but effective form of conservation. Its range is small compared with that of the Bewick's and Whoopers, but it holds a monopoly over Eastern Asia.

Jankowski is slightly larger than the Bewick's and has a longer, wider, thicker bill. This bill also is colored black and chrome, but the yellow patch comes down to and beyond the nostrils, intermediate in shape between those of the Whoopers and those of the Bewick's. The legs and feet are jet black. Only a trained ornithologist can distinguish this white, yellow, and black swan from its similar cousins in Europe. Oddly enough, it is rarely if ever depicted in the exquisite bird pictures of the Orient.

Late in March, flying out from the interior, these birds appear suddenly in large numbers along the coast of China. Here they gather and prepare for their spring flight to the North. Inhabiting a remote region where foreign ornithologists are not welcome, this little swan remains more or less a Slavic mystery.

Jankowski, like his small cousin the Bewick's, refuses to be domesticated and has only rarely and quite against his will been imported into other countries. At one time several pair were sent from China to the United States, but they declined to become naturalized. They fought and killed their companion ducks and geese and even the larger swans that ventured near. They were placed in solitary confinement for the sake of keeping the peace. The pen did build a nest but attacked her mate so violently that the experiment was abandoned.

Bewickii is polite about its refusal to be civilized, but *jankowski* pulls no punches and to this day is elusive and unknown.

There is a third swan to be catalogued here: the Immutable swan of the Baltic coast, the elegant *Cygnus immutabilis*. Immutable, meaning constant, unchanging, steadfast, refers not to its own lovely self but to its cygnets, hatched as they are pure white from pure white eggs and equipped with silvery gray legs and rosy bill. All other swan babies are gray, pretty enough at first but gradually growing duller and drabber until they eventually discard their early plumage, feather by feather, and become pure white like their parents. But Immutables are white from the start, the prettiest little creatures imaginable. Hans Christian Andersen must have been strangely ignorant of these glamorous swanlets so near his home country of Denmark. At least, there are no "ugly ducklings" among the Immutables. They are probably the most beautiful babies in all the world of birds.

The parent Immutable is somewhat smaller than the Mute and has a clear yellow bill with the addition of a black knob or "berry." The legs and feet are rosy pink instead of black. Ornithologists, who like to have everything in order, would prefer to call this "a domesticated and localized variant of *Cygnus olor*," but these unchangeable young baffle them. Try as they will, trace them back as far as records go, they find that the young Immutables have always been immutable and deserve a category of their own.

A strange swan this, content to remain in a restricted territory along the coast of the Baltic Sea, a region once known as East Prussia and Poland. The political shape of Poland has frequently changed through the centuries, and the range of this swan includes its one-time low coast line.

Indeed, it was originally known as the Polish swan. It can now be mated with the Mute swan to produce a satisfactory hybrid under that former name.

The low-lying coast of this practically tideless sea is a maze of inlets and lagoons and marshy inland lakes with exactly the shallow waters that swans naturally frequent. It is ideal swan country and there these gentle, harmless, beautiful birds live their quiet lives and raise their snowy youngsters, never troubling to migrate or change their range. Immutable might rightly be called a domestic swan, for it has firmly established itself and endeared itself to the inhabitants of this small and circumscribed area.

On the Island of Rugen, in particular, Immutables are an accepted and much-prized feature of the landscape, and their history goes back into the dim ages of legend and myth. Here, and possibly well over its small range, this swan, and not the familiar stork, is credited with bringing babies to human families, even though this is stork territory. Evidently the Immutable was thus honored on account of its hundred-miles-an-hour delivery, more than three times the speed of the stork.

✥ 5 ✥

The Wild Whistler

HOW MANY PEOPLE in the United States have seen our wild swans? Not the pampered, imported Mutes of city parks, but the glorious Trumpeters and their smaller cousins the Whistlers?

Who has heard them in the spring, passing overhead on their long flights to the North? The thin, flutelike whistling of the cygnets provides a counterpoint to the deep bass horns of the veterans: faint at first, deepening to a crescendo as they pass high overhead, becoming fainter and fainter as distance muffles their exultant notes.

The continent of North America possesses two species of wild swan: the Trumpeter, *Cygnus buccinator*, familiar to some because of its near-tragic history, and the Whistler, *Cygnus columbiana*, which is virtually unknown. Yet Whistlers are numerous, by no means to be considered a vanishing race.

Whistling swans are truly wild and very wary. They nest in the far North along the shores and islands of the Arctic Sea, flying so high on migration as to be practically invisible. They generally keep far inland, passing over the mountains and avoiding the perilous waterways where hunters lie in wait for ducks. This habit, coupled with the fact that they rarely alight on their journeys, has no doubt helped to preserve the race.

Certainly their great strength and the staying power of their eight-foot wing span have saved them from the fate of many other birds, for they can cover literally thousands of miles in one long, grueling flight without pausing to rest or feed. Even the cygnets keep up with the herd, placed between two veterans and supported by the slip stream of the bird ahead—no mean accomplishment for a six-months-old when the pace, with a favorable wind, sometimes reaches 100 miles an hour, as has been verified by the American naturalist Dr. D. G. Elliot and others. When overtaken by storm they rarely alight, but rise in unbroken flight above the weather as our commercial planes do.

Arthur Bent, author of *Life Histories of North American Wild Fowl*, declares that he had never even glimpsed a wild swan in flight until he was fifty years old. Then he experienced the thrill of his lifetime, for he saw:

> A flock of magnificent snow white birds glistening against
> the clear blue sky, their long necks pointing northward
> toward their polar home, their black feet trailing and

their translucent wings slowly beating the thin upper air
as they sped onwards on their long spring flight.

Once these swans were an accepted part of the landscape in places where they now no longer exist. They flew in
and wintered on lakes and marshes all through the western
and midwestern states as well as along the Pacific and Atlantic coasts. There are many descriptions by old-timers of
the tremendous herds of Whistlers that came to winter every
year in places which know them no more.

> The swans come in small flocks at intervals until they
> aggregate several hundred individuals . . . at the present
> time when we reached the lake there were 125 swans as
> we ascertained after frequent counts. They were grouped
> on the southwest shore of the lake immediately below the
> ranch where the fine mountain stream Alder Creek flows
> in. Some were standing on one leg in two or three inches
> of water, others floated asleep with their heads under
> their wings and, further away, watchful birds, constitut-
> ing a rear guard, were sailing about. . . . Mr. Williams
> informed us that no matter how much the swans might
> be disturbed they would always return to this place on
> account of the fresh water running in from the mountains.

This was written in 1911 by J. H. Holtman, but such
pleasant passages are the exception. Many excerpts from the
work of naturalists of the period make sad reading. Here is
an earlier account, author unknown:

> The swans were wont to feed along the marshy coves of
> the [Chesapeake] Bay and offered tempting shots. On
> windy, stormy days it was possible to creep up on them
> through the marsh near enough to get a shot. Approach-
> ing swans on the open water was a difficult proposition,
> especially if they were surrounded, as they often were,
> by watchful geese. . . . In winter, boats covered with
> blocks of ice and manned by gunners dressed in white

could sometimes be paddled or allowed to drift within gunshot of a feeding flock.

Another sportsman, also unidentified, glories in fog which enables him to get within easy range. A third gleefully describes five swans killed with one blast of a heavy gun, of course hidden from sight. Unfortunately, swans seem to have no sense of smell. They can detect an enemy only by sight or sound.

As late as 1912 J. H. Fleming described an orgy of slaughter that occurred in what is aptly called the Niagara Swan Trap. Here a vast herd of swans was caught in the rapids and, unable to take flight between the narrow banks of the river, was swept over the falls. Many were killed in the rush of the water, others were maimed in the whirlpools which hurled them against the rocks or crushed them against floating ice. As soon as the struggling survivors, unable to fly on account of their injuries, battled their way into smoother waters, a mob of men and boys shot, beat, and clubbed the exhausted birds to death. Not one escaped.

This case was no exception. There were many records of wanton wholesale destruction, often described with great gusto. An insatiable desire to kill something swift and beautiful seems to have possessed the minds of many men, and it is a marvel that any of our spectacular birds have survived until now.

The perils of civilization are not the only dangers our wild swans have to meet. Even in their remote nesting grounds in the frozen north they are still at the merciless mercy of Man. Late in August when the cygnets are not yet fully fledged, the parent birds lose their strong flight feathers in one quick molt and become helplessly earth-bound during a hazardous two or three weeks. It is at this time that they fall victims to the Eskimos and other natives who rely on them for food and clothing. These people have never been known to kill for sport, and the Whistlers would have been able to maintain their numbers if they had had to contend only with such hunters. In fact, the Whistler has survived in spite of a persecution under which the stronger but less wary Trumpeter all but succumbed.

The Whistler is, in reality, a small replica of this bigger swan. It is about five feet in length against the Trumpeter's five foot six and, while the Whistler's wing span measures seven to eight feet, the Trumpeter's sometimes reaches the tremendous spread of nine and, it is rumored, ten feet. The Whistler is pure white as all the northern swans are, and it has the usual black bill and feet. It is distinguishable from the Trumpeter by a small yellow patch in front of the eye. However, all Whistlers do not have this distinctive mark and, in former days, there seems to have been some confusion. Stories of the fabulous numbers of Trumpeters probably included this commoner species.

In the United States where most of these birds pass

the winter, they wisely frequent the great wild-fowl refuges provided by federal and state governments and various conservation societies. Occasionally they may be seen on open sloughs and lakes where they are safer than formerly, for the penalty for killing a swan of any kind is $500 plus six months in jail. Not only the swans, but the geese and ducks as well seem to realize this, for it is noticeable that, in unprotected areas where swans are present, ducks and geese cluster around them.

Birds are sometimes considered stupid by people who study their reactions from a human viewpoint. But they belong to a creation apart from ours, living within the circle of a great natural law. Their minds are uncluttered with irrelevant matters which to us seem important. They are quick to see and understand anything that pertains to their own welfare. Thus they will ignore a plane zooming and

sputtering across the sky. But let a silent hawk appear like a pinpoint, and its prospective victims are instantly on the alert. The big swans have, as earlier mentioned, their natural enemies: coyotes, foxes, weasels, eagles, ravens, even crows and big predatory sea gulls, and possibly the egg-destroying loon, as recorded in England. These they recognize and cope with. But Man is still the unpredictable adversary.

Sometimes an audacious swan will practice a little persecution himself. A short while ago newspapers carried a story from Oregon, where a Whistler was making himself a nuisance by chasing cows on a dairy farm. He found it great fun to stampede the inoffending cattle whenever they approached the feeding troughs, and many wounded themselves in their terrified efforts to evade him. After two seasons of this behavior, he was caught with a lure of bread crusts. Then his wings were cut and in disgrace he was shipped to a nearby zoo. The following year, his wings grown again, he was back at the same place and, finding no cows, he started after the ducks. What sport that was! Finally he was removed to a zoo in Northern California where he is still chasing ducks.

The usual bird's nest serves only as a cradle, but a swan's nest can rightly be called its home, for, long after the eggs have ben incubated, the family returns to it each night to rest and sleep. Each year they remodel and repair it, keeping it like the old family mansion.

The nest of the Whistlers resembles the structures built by others of their race: a huge mound of grass, moss, sticks, and reeds built up to a safe height from the ground with a depression in the middle which is lined with soft swan's-down and, in regions where it can be found, loose dry moss. If possible a small island is chosen as the site, or the low bank of a river or lakelet. The nest is artfully concealed not

only from Man but also from nonhuman prowlers, while the eggs are carefully covered with leaves and moss when both parents are absent. Over the years a nest may become six feet across, raised three feet from the ground.

The eggs are creamy brown in color, with a finely granulated shell that is soon nest-stained. The cygnets hatch out after about forty days. They are downy and fluffy, with sparkling dark brown eyes and pale pink-buff-color bills and feet. Precocious, they run around as soon as they have recovered from the ordeal of breaking out of the shell. Although they can pick up grass and bits of weeds with their tender bills and can paddle around in the shallow water, they have to be trained to be swans.

Sometimes deep snow covers the ground around the nest. This is an additional safeguard if civilization is near, and it does them no harm. Soon the sun is shining all day and practically all night, and there is plenty of time for education and play. Opportunities for observing the young of the Whistler have not been many, but there can be no doubt that they are trained in much the same way as the Mute cygnets are, perhaps even more intensively.

They retain their downy plumage until the end of September, when the bill is purplish with a dark "nail" on the tip and the gape, or outline, of the upper mandible is black. The plumage by then is a light sooty brown with lead color on the head and neck and a silvery gray luster on the newly grown flight feathers. But there is still an air of adolescent gaucherie, and the eyes which are now hazel are confidingly innocent.

A Whistler swan of either sex takes from four to five years to attain maturity. A yearling, though it can take part in the long flights to and from winter quarters, is still only about a third the size of its parents and may weigh as little as ten pounds against the thirty pounds of a full-grown cob.

Even when fully grown and a creature of beauty, the youngster is not ready to choose a lifelong mate. A young cob may set his fancy on some glamorous pen as big and beautiful as himself, but three or four years must elapse before they actually mate and start the serious business of raising a family. The family is always small to start with, not more than four or, at the most, five cygnets.

The diet is mostly vegetarian, though a certain type of soft fresh-water snail is a favorite food. They also eat the spawn of fish and frogs, but the peculiar formation of their long necks makes it impossible for them to eat marketable fish. They can eat water worms and large insects, particularly the predatory water beetles that prey on the minute young of edible fish.

Swans feed as ducks and geese do, by reaching down to the bottom of the lake and gleaning the roots and shoots found there. Complaints have been made that, in their winter quarters, they pull up the wild celery and various grasses by the roots, thus destroying valuable duck food, to the disgust of hunters to whom ducks are legitimate prey while swans are a tantalizing taboo. Nevertheless, this grievance has been investigated and disproved. Indeed, it has been found that these succulent foods increase where swans do their type of pruning.

The why and the how of migration are still unsolved. We can simply envy these birds their untrammeled trips in pursuit of the sun.

Before venturing on the southward journey in the early fall, not only the dusky cygnets but the wide-winged adults as well practice flying. They rise from the water in small parties and take a swift course around and around the lake or up and down the river. A compact group flying in close formation circles the lake several times and alights on the surface so close together and with such perfect timing that one wonders at the control they must exercise over their plump thirty-pound bodies. They never collide or touch wings, and all alight with a minimum of splash and fuss.

When every one, down to the youngest cygnet, is fit and ready, places in line are allotted. The strongest and wisest of the veterans takes off first, and the others follow, one after the other, flying silently and low, gradually rising and speeding, their voices raised in chorus like a fanfare of an orchestra. Soon they steady down to a pace they can maintain, their long necks stretched to full length, undulating slightly with the tremendous effort, their black feet close to their snowy flanks, extending to just beyond the tail, their bodies streamlined, waxed to a glistening nonresistance, their wide wings beating slowly and regularly with an unwavering power and drive.

One can imagine the ecstasy of the cygnets on this their

The Wild Whistler

first adventure, their smaller wings faithfully following the sweeping strokes of the old-timer in the lead. Their piping flutelike voices sound in heady exultation as they rise and rise into the wine of the upper air. The long line becomes a precisely streamlined V, each bird alert and aware, wing-beats wafting them along in a mighty surging unit of concerted effort.

High and yet higher they rise, for the mountains are ahead. Minute dazzling crystals of ice frost their wing tips and are shaken off in a glitter of swirling diamonds with each sweep. The clouds are below them, towering masses of cumulus, white as themselves but reaching down in shades of purple and blue to where the mountain lakes shine. Higher and higher and even higher they fly. The sun is setting now, and the sky is a deeper and deeper ultramarine. Now it is velvet purple, and the stars are hanging in the rarefied air.

The mountains are passed at last. Down now, slowly, slowly down. The clouds are gone, soon the moon will rise and the earth will appear again, dark and perfumed, rolling

inexorably sunward, bearing its faintly gleaming lakes and rivers and the blurred, golden lights of perilous cities.

On and on and on. Their wings are not yet tired. The noblest of them all is leading them. Not the grand old cob who started the flight—he is resting, swinging along in the stream at the rear—but another as strong and competent spells him for a while.

Now the old cob surges forward to take the lead again. The pace is checked. The long necks bear slightly downward as glimmering water appears below. It rises to meet them in the half light with the heady scent of the marshland and the faint gaggling of friendly water birds. Down they all drift like a flurry of snowflakes. Their wings curve forward, their feet thrust out to check their landing.

The water at last, cool and shimmering with reflected stars, and the first hint of the dawn is in the sky. They are down. They are safe. They are tired, so tired.

The Wild Whistler

In the morning what a chorus! Greetings, congratulations, and bursts of wood-wind melody, while they preen and gossip and take snatches of sleep. Their friends the geese are here. They will associate with them all winter, though they never join in migration. The plump little ducks are here, too, crowding around the newcomers at feeding time, gleaning the tastier bits from deep water which the big birds loosen and discard.

The swans rest and relax. They swim around, they fly a little, they plunge their long necks into the water to feed, they preen their snowy feathers, and they sleep with long necks laid along their backs. Often a black foot is hitched up on one side. For this position the leg must first be extended backward and sideways, with web spread out for drying before it is thrust under the immaculate feathers.

Winter is the time to let the troublesome world go by. Each family, cob, pen, and cygnets, will remain closely together until the old birds nest again in the spring, and, even after that there will be friendly contact between parents and offspring, for the family relationship continues to be strong in all members of this genus.

The swans will remain on vacation down south in the United States all winter if they are not disturbed. They will return again and again to this haven of their choice, this small gleaming pinpoint on the vast dark surface of the earth, reached and located unerringly each year after the grueling flight of over a thousand miles.

Whistling swans are wise, even among birds of a wise race. They time their northward flight later than most of the waterfowl and usually manage to avoid the fateful blizzards of early spring.

When spring is in the air once more they become restless. They gather in large groups and make a real business of preening and oiling their feathers, like athletes in training. They call to one another, keeping up a constant conversation as if discussing plans and directions for the coming flight to their distant nesting grounds.

At a given signal and with loud calls they all mount into the air, taking off against the wind in a whirring surge of wings. Each bird takes its apportioned place in the long lines as they wing up and away toward their real home, the North.

The music of swans in flight is one of the wildest in Nature. The windpipe of an adult Whistler measures sometimes as much as five feet in length and, doubled and looped around the breastbone, it gives the deep resonance often audible at a distance of two miles.

When the North calls, you may imagine these great wild ones singing, in the lines of Patrick Chalmers:

> We from the North came from frozen sea-sources,
> We to the North turn from whence we came forth,
> We the Wild Whistlers, like stars in our courses,
> Pass in the dawn to our Homeland, the North.

⁂ 6 ⁂

The Great Trumpeter

UNTIL the middle of the last century the great Trumpeter, *Cygnus buccinator,* the prince of swans, was the glory of the western flyways. This magnificent bird was the prevailing swan in Washington, Oregon, and California. It ranged over much of the interior of North America, nesting in Canada and in the northwestern states and even in a few areas east of the Mississippi River. In the old days the Trumpeter could be seen and certainly heard throughout the northern states, and the clanging bugling cry of these birds in flight was a familiar sound to the early settlers. The clarion notes were said to carry over a distance of two miles. As a flight passed overhead, the sound rolled and re-echoed and reverberated to a crescendo, rising and rising in volume, then slowly dying away to a faint note like the winding of a huntsman's horn as the birds sped away out of sight.

The Latin name of these swans is derived from this trumpeting call, the buccinator being a thin muscle in the human cheek used for the blowing of a horn or trumpet.

The Trumpeter swan, female as well as male, measures around five feet six inches from bill to tail, against the five feet of most other wild swans. Its wingspread is all of eight feet, and a measurement as great as ten feet has been recorded. The neck is exceedingly long and slender, with twenty-nine vertebrae, and it is always held perfectly erect except during feeding or sleeping. The plumage of the adult is pure white, the bill and large webbed feet are uniformly black. The Whistler, which closely resembles it except for size, has a distinguishing small patch of yellow in front of the eye. There is no need to search for this identification when you see a Trumpeter, however, for you will know that no other swan can be so big and so beautiful. The cygnets are unmistakable too, their feet being yellow and black while those of the Whistler youngsters are pinkish, maturing to gray-purple.

The real distinction of this swan of all swans is of course its voice. Trumpet is hardly the word to describe the timbre of its notes, which are loud and clear but by no means brassy. They suggest more the mellow tones of the wood wind, from the clarinet pipings of the cygnets to veterans' deep bassoon. It is the greatest voice in all the swan family. The Whistlers, with their five-foot windpipes looped beneath the breastbone, cannot compete, for the Trumpeter's neck is longer, and its windpipe is looped not only once but twice, augmenting the volume and the resonance of the notes.

Trumpeters used to fly lower than their wise cousins the Whistlers and they followed the waterways where they fell easy prey to duck hunters. Their habit of alighting to feed and rest near areas of cultivation also contributed to their undoing, for the dazzlingly white birds were slaughtered indiscriminately. Old records reveal that in cases where storm-driven birds were forced to alight, the entire population of men and boys in a nearby town turned out to shoot or club them to death, while they were exhausted and helpless. For sport's sake the tough and uneatable old ones were destroyed with the young..

These Trumpeters, big and powerful as they were, seem never to have had the wit and staying power of the Whistlers. They quickly succumbed to conditions over which the smaller birds triumphed. In the earliest days they too nested in the Arctic regions and were taken by the Eskimos each summer at the time when they lost their flight feathers before migration. They seem to have been the heaviest sufferers during the fur-trading period around the middle of the last

century, when the settlers of the Northlands developed a lucrative business selling the skins of various birds to the fur traders. Swan skins were the most marketable and profitable; the skins of Trumpeters, being bigger and heavier, fetched the best price of all. It is recorded that between 1853 and 1877 the Hudson Bay Company alone sold 17,671 swan skins, and most of these are believed to have been of the Trumpeter.

The trade continued briskly until in 1918, the Migratory Treaty banned all traffic in wild birds. By that time the Trumpeter was almost extinct. A few individuals remained in remote districts of Canada and Alaska, and remnants survived on the borders of Montana and Idaho.

At the turn of the century a new use for swans was discovered, and the flightless cygnets were caught and shipped to buyers all over the world, at the rewarding price of $75 per head. Most of them were destined for zoos, some for parks and private estates, but it is a strange fact that they never succeeded in establishing themselves anywhere but in a limited area of North America. The popularity of swans saved the Trumpeters from complete annihilation for, in order to maintain the valuable supply of young, merchants

had to allow the parent birds to live and raise their families.

It was in the mid-forties that Ralph Edwardes and his daughter Trudy, pioneers in Canada's wild Northwest, found themselves the proud intimates of a herd of some two dozen Trumpeter swans that wintered on their property at Lonesome Lake, near Atnarko, in Alaska. The Canadian Government, hearing of this hitherto unknown herd, appointed them wardens and provided them with grain for winter feeding. Trudy at the age of thirteen took over the task of feeding and caring for them, and she is probably the only person from whose hand such wild swans ever fed. Their numbers increased under her care.

When a gift of wild swans to the then princess Elizabeth of England was planned, Ottawa's officials decided that the only place such wary birds could be captured was Lonesome Lake, and that the only person who could capture them was Trudy Edwardes. A large trap was set up, and Trudy herself enticed the semitame birds inside with a scattering of barley. Five beautiful and rare Trumpeters were obtained in this manner and shipped by fast plane to England. Trudy never forgave herself for her treachery, and it seemed that the rest of the swans at Lonesome Lake would not forgive her either. It was four long years before they would again eat out of her hand.

The five trumpeters sent to England are now established at Peter Scott's celebrated Wildfowl Trust on the Bristol Channel. A sixth bird was soon procured, and therefore he has three healthy pairs. They are about fourteen years old at this writing, and though several nests have been built and even a few eggs laid, no cygnets have as yet been raised. Next spring the swans will be moved to a secluded corner of the refuge where they will not be disturbed by visitors. Trumpeter swans are still sensitive to interference even after more than twenty-five years of protection.

The humane Migratory Treaty was not sufficient to ensure the wild Trumpeter's protection, for there were other circumstances that contributed to its decline, the most menacing being civilization itself. The birds had abandoned their far northern habitat, and their nesting grounds in the United States grew more and more restricted as land was reclaimed and settled, for their territory now lay within the highly cultivated sections of the Plains and the Great Lakes. Here swamps were drained and built upon, until only a small portion of marshy country within the states of Montana, Idaho, Wyoming, and Colorado remained to them.

By 1935 an actual count showed only seventy-three individual Trumpeters surviving. Then at last people became determined that this magnificent swan, the biggest water bird in the United States (if not in the whole world), should not be allowed to become extinct like the passenger pigeon and the Carolina parakeet. The National Audubon Society had already devoted thirty years of publicity on behalf of threatened wild fowl. Inspired and supported by the interest and sympathy finally aroused in the public, a constructive campaign was started by George Wright and Ben Thomson of the National Park Service. They had begun in 1900 to try to make people realize the plight of the swans. The Director of the Fish and Wildlife Service, Jan N. Darling (known to all as Ding Darling), was perhaps the originator of the workable plan, and then the anonymous warmhearted public contributed their dollars to the purchase price of appropriate land.

In the late 1920's George Wright and his associates in the National Park Service found that the few survivors of the Trumpeter race nesting in the Yellowstone area were barely holding their own. Drastic measures were necessary if these swans were to be preserved for posterity. In scouting for a suitable location for a sanctuary, Wright discovered the Red Rock Lakes area some fifty miles west of Yellowstone Park in a high valley among the mountains. In this valley a remnant of breeding swans had congregated, and its swamps and marshes were the refuge of innumerable other migratory waterfowl. It was also the mecca of trigger-happy hunters, a fact which accounted in part for the yearly decrease of the swan population.

Mr. Darling, then the head of the Department of Biological Survey, made a personal investigation, with the result that the area was set aside and the Refuge established early in 1935. This was the turning point, and soon the refuge was filled with breeding swans.

The site of this sanctuary was indeed well chosen. The area extends over 40,000 acres and consists largely of marshy meadows studded with shallow lakes, a swan's ideal nesting place. There is abundant water even in the driest season, since three streams enter the Refuge: Red Rock Creek, Elk Springs Creek, and Odel Creek. In the lakes there is ample vegetation suitable for long-neck feeding. Winter brings heavy snow to the region, but at the far eastern side there are perennial warm springs that provide open water even in the severest weather. Therefore the birds feel no compulsion to migrate to warmer quarters.

The Trumpeter swans are now protected and know it. Rarely do they fly outside the restricted area of the Refuge, where they are fed a ration of grain when the weather becomes too severe for their natural feeding. However, a few do venture over the mountains into Yellowstone Park and the Henry's Fork or other sheltered tributaries of the Snake River in northeastern Idaho, where they find not only the food but the isolation they require. Lately, under the auspices of the National Audubon Society, several pairs have been established on Lake Malheur in Oregon and on Ruby Lake in Nevada, in the hope of increasing their range. It is also planned to establish forty young birds each year in various other selected spots.

This was, no doubt, the dream of the first conservationists. Now it is being realized beyond their most optimistic hopes.

Trumpeters require isolation for their nesting, and their clutch of eggs is small, three to five against the round dozen of the prolific Mute. With little danger from natural causes, the colony is flourishing. In their new home the Trumpeters conform to the same habits as their wild brethren, with the exception of the spring and fall migration. They mate for life, they dance for joy during the mating season, they build and remodel their nests and train their cygnets to be not just swans but Trumpeter swans.

The cob does not share in the incubation as the Mute cob does. Usually he just stands near the nest. With a long memory of persecution he can be particularly fierce and dangerous at such times, while both cob and pen display courage beyond their size and strength. Once a huge bull moose in the Yellowstone section of the Refuge ventured too near an incubating pen. The infuriated cob attacked him, beating him with wings and bill and feet, until the moose retreated at an ignominious gallop.

Even in the Refuge these swans seem to remember their wild days and unrelenting fight for survival, for they still choose to build their nests on small islands or on hummocks surrounded by water. The pen is still a true denizen of the wild, always on the alert, her jet eyes watchful, her long neck erect even while she is on the nest. As formerly, when she leaves to feed she covers her precious eggs with grass or moss, as though to guard them against eagles and ravens and the four-footed predators of earlier days.

The thirty-five- or forty-day incubation period is a long day-and-night chore for the pen.

The very young cygnets reverse the usual order of diet. They first feed on fresh-water shrimp and small aquatic insects, graduating to the vegetable matter that provides their future staple food.

They weigh only about eight ounces when first hatched in June. They grow rapidly, and by early autumn many of them have attained a weight of fifteen pounds. They can be seen exercising their wings long before they venture on their first flight, and they propel their heavy bodies over the water with large running feet until at last they are airborne and away.

The youngsters lead a carefree existence for the first few years. They do not mate until they are at least three years old, and even then they do not start a family for another year or two. They have a long life before them now and, with any luck, each pair, given time and opportunity, can raise a hundred young. If all goes well, the areas at present allotted to them may prove too restricted. Already the Refuge has reached saturation point and the birds are being colonized on nearby lakes and rivers. Soon they may have to launch out on their own and rediscover ancient haunts.

The 1962 census for Trumpeter swans in the United States reported a count of 1,581 individuals. A few years ago, however, the number of Trumpeters in the region of the Refuge was diminishing instead of increasing. There were

642 birds in 1954, only 590 in 1955, 588 in 1956, despite the most devoted supervision. The cause? Largely hunters. Certain types of hunters seem to be immune to education or suggestion. I have permission to quote a passage from Keith Barrette's thoughtful article in *Nature Magazine*, "A Trumpeter Swan Winter Resort":

> Almost every hunting season several swans fall victim to trigger-happy incompetents with shotguns. No doubt part of this is indiscriminate shooting, but some is malicious destruction. This may, in part, account for the decline in numbers. . . . Just why anyone would want, willfully, to destroy one of these great birds is difficult to imagine. As game birds they are completely worthless but, as an esthetic part of our national heritage, the Trumpeter is without price. Threats of fine and incarceration ($500 plus six months' imprisonment) do not seem to deter these vandals. . . . With the approach of the water-fowl season, Federal and Idaho conservation officials keep anxious eyes and constant vigil. Not until the hunting season ends and the winter begins to wane, do these keepers of our wild life breathe easier, but they are admittedly alarmed over this needless drain on the still low population of America's Trumpeters.

Hunters, too shortsighted, too ignorant, too indifferent to distinguish a long-necked, pure white, full-sized swan from a small white goose with jet-black wing tips, are likely to shoot any bird they see outside the Refuge, claiming to mistake it for a snow goose. To prevent these "mistakes," a supplementary law has been passed. It is now illegal to shoot any goose of any kind whatever in the sections of Montana, Wyoming, and Idaho bordering on the Refuge. Here is a case of real cooperation among the states.

Actual shooting is not the only trouble. The greatest menace to swans in a restricted area is lead poisoning caused by the pellets from shotguns, which fall into the shallow lakes and are swallowed by the birds as they feed along the bottom. This results in a slow and inevitable death, to which the Trumpeter especially is prone. This is a danger wherever hunters abound, even though they may be careful and law-abiding.

There is still a herd of Trumpeters in existence in Canada's Northwest, and they seem to be maintaining their numbers under natural conditions. Swans around Grand Prairie, Alberta, nest close to the dwellings and are accustomed to people. One pair established themselves in a slough just behind the airport, and the roar of the four-engined planes coming in low for a landing seemed not to worry them at all. Many seem almost tame, and the inhabitants of the region look upon them with real affection. Some declare that they would report their own relatives if they were caught shooting a swan. Recently a railroad man shot a swan "by mistake for a goose" and was turned over to the police by his irate co-workers. He was charged the maximum fine.

Though these swans object to the too-close proximity of geese, they allow ducks to nest within a few feet of their own massive structures. All live in peace except the scrappy

red-winged blackbird, who resents any approach to his territory among the reeds. With scarlet shoulders spread like a flaming cape, he divebombs the big white enemies, even pecking them on the head if they do not move away fast enough.

The swans in this area can be approached closely on the water, but the pen will quietly leave the nest if sighted and will not return until the boat has left the lake. If her cygnets are already hatched she will scatter them and hide them until danger is past. It is said that the Trumpeter's neck will curve gracefully when he is completely relaxed but that at the slightest alarm it will stiffen up. When he is angry the neck is sharply bent with the head thrust low and forward, sometimes resting on the water.

Trumpeter swans weigh up to forty pounds and have difficulty in taking off. The adults prefer dry land rather than water as a runway. When preparing to fly, they pump their heads up and down and trumpet loudly, taking off against the wind with running feet and heavily flapping wings. They alight into the wind, braking with their wings and feet and allowing themselves plenty of space. In nesting time the adults rarely fly. Swans seen in flight at this time are usually immatures or nonbreeders.

Although they breed around Lake Saskatoon, the Trumpeters of Canada, unlike the herds of the Yellowstone, migrate in winter to the milder coastal area. A few remain and have been known to die of hunger on remote frozen lakes where it was not possible to supply them with supplementary grain. A herd of about a thousand is to be found in Alaska, principally in the Kenai Peninsula and the valley of the Yukon. These birds fly down into Canada in the winter, bringing the total population up to slightly over fifteen hundred.

On the Yellowstone Refuge the swans are now trying

their wings and venturing into unrestricted territory. This is, of course, an encouraging sign, for they cannot recover their true untrammeled characteristics while confined to an increasingly congested area.

Recently a swan flew into the Red Rock Refuge accompanied by four cygnets, all banded in Canada. The adult swan, unhappily, was dead when found, but she wore on her leg a numbered band for Saskatoon Lake, near Grand Prairie, Alberta. The banded youngsters were in good condition after a flight of 850 miles.

Let us hope that these wilder Canadian birds will find the United States a pleasant wintering resort and join the resident herds. This may induce the swans of the Refuge to migrate north for the nesting season as they did in the days before the Great Persecution.

ॐ 7 ॐ

In South America

THERE IS a sharp division of opinion among those who admire swans. In the Northern Hemisphere a swan is expected
to be white, and the purest alabaster white at that, while in
Australia and New Zealand a swan is not a swan unless it
is black, and as black as possible. But in South America we
find a swan that might be called a compromise: *Cygnus
nigro collis* has a snowy body and a completely black neck.

Swans have for so long been associated with northern
lands that you may be rather surprised to realize that there

is one peculiar to South America. Yet what continent is better suited to a large water bird? Here are enormous swamp-bordered rivers, huge tracts of marshland, and miles of lush country seldom, if ever, invaded by Man. Here the blight of civilization is still confined to relatively small areas, leaving vast territories unexploited. What more could a swan desire?

The Black-necked swan is to be found all through the south from coast to coast, a winter visitor only north of Latitude 35. In 1833 Charles Darwin observed it in Chile "in a deep inlet in the company of seals and otters." And W. H. Hudson writes in his *Idle Days in Patagonia* that "far out in the middle of the swift blue current floated flocks of blacknecked swans, their white plumage shining like foam in the sunlight." These birds, partial to the brackish waters of lagoons and estuaries, are still numerous near the coast. They are most common on open lakes and marshlands, however, and congregate in large flocks at nesting time, when each pair claims a territory and defends it in true swan fashion.

This is a shy bird and very cautious, though it has little reason to be. The Black-neck is not beset with the dangers encountered by other swans. Its flesh is black and exceedingly rank, quite unfit for human food, and therefore it is never hunted for game. Moreover, the primitive natives of the remoter districts have always considered the taking of life except for food an actual crime.

Nigro collis is little larger than the dainty Bewick's; the pen is smaller than the cob and has a shorter neck. The body is longer and the wings wider and rounder than the northern swan's, while the legs are very short and set far back, making the walk an ungainly waddle. When on the wing it is swift and strong, though it migrates only from the northern to the southern range of its territory, flying south in the spring and north in the fall. Like most swans it is a noisy bird, but the noise it produces is a pleasant musical whistle quickly repeated—not at all like the haunting cry of its white brethren. On the ground it converses in gentle gossipy syllables and has a varied vocabulary.

There is no mistaking the Black-neck in any company, even apart from its striking plumage. It is the only swan other than the all-black swan of Australia and the familiar Mute to curve its neck and arch its wings when swimming. Its shape is long and narrow with pointed tail, while the pink and gray bill is small and flaunts a large double-lobed knob or "berry" of vivid red. In color the legs are pale buff-pink. A clear white line curves back from the eye through the black plumage, inconspicuous in the young but growing wider and longer with age until, in the veteran, it

forms a narrow band almost meeting at the back of the head. The neck and head are otherwise uniformly black, and that color ends abruptly where it meets the white of the shoulder.

This swan builds a nest among the reeds and rushes, always near shallow water. Incubation lasts over a month, and the pen does all the brooding. The cob stands guard and attacks any intruder with curved neck thrust forward and wings raised threateningly. When the pen leaves the nest to relax or feed or stretch her legs, even though she may be away for a long period she does not bother to cover the eggs, as other swans do. Her eggs have a high gloss and are deep cream in color. She lays four, at most five, but if the clutch is accidentally destroyed she will cheerfully lay again and yet again, determined to raise a family.

When at last the eggs crack and the nestlings emerge, the vigil proves to have been worthwhile. Baby *nigro collis* are among the most attractive of young cygnets, little puffs of oyster white which fluffs right down to the nostrils of their jet-black bills. Their stumpy legs and spreading webbed feet are black to match.

These cygnets are timid youngsters. They remain under their mother's wings all the first day. On the second day they venture shyly out to feed and swim a little, a mere dabble of a first bath. Then they all climb up on the parents' backs and nestle deep between the slightly busked wings. Only after a week do they dare to descend, except briefly, for meals. Even when they have finally summoned the courage to swim alone, they hastily climb back to hide in their feathery refuge at the slightest alarm. Each evening they take shelter under their parents' wings, and they continue to do this until they seem altogether too big to be so babied.

As in the case of other swans, their food is mainly plant life gleaned from the bottom of shallow pools. The neck is articulated to serve this purpose, and the cygnets are taught to choose the good and reject the bad. Indeed, the thorough training parallels that of the Mutes. Young Black-necks mature more rapidly than their northern cousins and attain a more or less adult plumage in one year. At first they are not as strikingly beautiful as their parents, the black being merely seal brown and the bill lacking the red frontal. After they are fully grown they are still not ready to mate for a year or two. They do not start to raise a family until they are three or four years old.

Black-necks are exceedingly tolerant of the duck family, which they are never known to molest, but for some reason they heartily show their dislike of geese when they are associated with them in captivity. Otherwise these attractive swans take readily to captivity and a life of ease, adjusting to climate and environment with little difficulty. They are extremely hardy and can sleep serenely on an ice-locked lake or can occupy a limited body of water with no ill results. For this reason they are often seen with the Mute swans on park lakes where they are doubtless looked upon as freaks by the general public.

They were not introduced into Europe until the middle of the nineteenth century. A live pair reached the Antwerp Zoo in 1846, and a pair of the resulting cygnets was bought as a present for the Earl of Derby in England. He added them to his remarkable collection of exotic birds on his estate at Knowsley. Unfortunately, at his death his collection was scattered. Some of the Black-necks were sent to the London Zoological Gardens, and some to the lake in St. James Park where their descendants can still be seen.

At about the same time a Dutchman, M. Polivet, was the first private individual on the continent to possess a pair. At his death, too, the swans were sold, this time to the Antwerp Zoo, which paid the surprising sum, for those days, of two thousand francs apiece. Though the value of the franc at that time made it a stiff price, it proved a rare bargain, for the following year the couple produced five healthy cygnets and, in turn, these cygnets paired and started to raise additional families. The second year the original pen died mysteriously while incubating, and her clutch was abandoned. But the old cob, after an interval, paired off with one of the younger cygnets—a most unusual proceeding for a swan.

The change of hemisphere and subsequent reversal of the seasons sometimes muddles the swans' sense of timing, not just temporarily but permanently. In captivity in the north they mate and nest at any time, sometimes choosing to hatch out their young in the depths of winter, with sad results. However, they are extremely prolific and, even in captivity, the pen lays a second clutch of four or five eggs if the first is taken away and placed under a goose. One wonders how the first brood regard their foster mother, geese being natural enemies of this type of swan.

In their native haunts Black-necks feed largely on green vegetation with a variation of beetles and snails. But when tamed they have a strong liking for cooked rice and, of course, other grains. They will eat almost anything of that nature. In fact, they are the most tractable of all the swan family, even more so than the time-honored Mute, for they are rarely quarrelsome and have little urge to migrate. It is said that a pair of adults can be kept in health and happiness on a pool no bigger than thirty by fifteen yards and that the pen will start laying at three years of age. These birds are graceful as they swim, and in flight their wings produce a pleasant whistling sound unlike the swish and throb of others of their kind.

The southern part of South America is the home of another genus, the *Coscoroba coscoroba*, a strange bird that supplies the present-day link between the swans and geese.

To the uninitiated this handsome bird looks just like another swan. But it is different in an elusive, perplexing way. It is smaller, its tail is short and rounded, and its long legs are set near the middle of the body instead of far to the rear as is usual with the cygnus family. Thus it walks like a goose, without the ungainly roll and lurch of a true swan. The general coloring is different too, for, though the bird is white, the wings are surprisingly tipped with black and the bill, which is slightly flattened at the tip like the bill of a duck, is rosy pink with a white "nail." The legs and the large feet are pink also, and the eye of the male is so light as to appear to be white with a pink eyelid. The female's eye is a ruddy chestnut brown. Except for size and length of neck and bill, the bird could be an exaggerated snow goose.

It is odd that Charles Darwin in his *Voyage of the Beagle* did not mention this extraordinary bird, for he explored the regions where even now it is commonly seen. One would expect to find in his voluminous diary at least several pages devoted to the description of a bird so big and unique. Even the striking and unusual Black-neck, at that time unknown to Europe and certainly new to Darwin, rates only a casual mention under "Chile and the Chonon Islands" (Chapter XIII):

We also saw a pair of the beautiful Black-necked swans.

The Coscoroba is wild and very timid, despite its commanding size. It is found in large numbers in certain areas while in other places, apparently equally desirable, it is absent. This is peculiar, for it walks and flies with great ease

and is able to rise straight from the ground as ducks do, because of its longer and more centrally placed legs. It has not the grace of the true swan on the water, though it does swim with dignity, neck held straight and bill pointing down. It never arches its wings as the Black-neck does. Therefore the black primaries appear only as a contrasting line until the bird opens its pinions and takes wing. Then the spectacle is breath-taking, for the take-off is singularly graceful.

Like the Black-neck the Coscoroba is a noisy bird, particularly when on the wing. Its voice, like itself, is unique and is said to resemble the four syllables of its name, the first note long and high, the others shorter and on a descending scale. W. H. Hudson, in his account of a boyhood spent in the Argentine, remarks:

> . . . the trumpeting of the great Coscoroba swan was not heard at a great distance, its notes being without the shrill quality of the larger water-birds.

This seems most unswanlike, and it is true that the Coscoroba lacks the long looped windpipe found in other varieties of the race.

Nesting time for Coscorobas is in the austral spring, which corresponds with the autumn season of northern lands, any time between late September and early December. It is preceded by a gay nuptial dance. The birds raise their rounded black-tipped wings and pirouette tiptoe on their large feet while they move their heads quickly backward and forward, uttering their special cry. The pen is just as expert as the cob. Indeed, you can hardly tell them apart, as the plumage is identical. The female is said to be smaller, but this is not always the case.

Migration for these birds is irregular, though most of the nesting seems to occur in the south, even as far south as the inhospitable Straits of Magellan. The nest is often placed actually in the water and has the usual structure, built up of reeds and stems with efficient drainage below and a deep hollow lined with soft grass and down.

The eggs are white and almost round, and the nestlings emerge in November or even as late as January after the usual month-long incubation. The pen does all the incubating, while the faithful cob keeps watch. Later he takes full share in the education of the extraordinary little brood.

At first sight it seems hard to believe that these Coscoroba babies are cygnets at all, for their plumage is boldly patterned and they look more like large ducklings. Indeed they closely resemble the young of the so-called Whistling duck which, in its turn, is not a duck at all but is deviously connected with the swan family. A description of a Coscoroba cygnet is a description of a Whistling duckling except for size.

Shaped like an infant swan, it is grayish white in color

with a pure white band across the back of the head. This band is bisected by a narrow black line which runs down the nape, broadening and continuing all the way to the rump. In addition there is a distinct black patch on the crown of the head and an area of black around each eye. The whole effect, except for the gray-and-rose-colored bill and the long silvery legs, is that of an overgrown duckling of indeterminate breed.

This youngster so closely approximates the young of the Whistling duck that a question arises: what are the true antecedents of the Coscoroba? Here we glance at the fossil swan found on the Island of Malta, and we see that

it resembles the Coscoroba more closely than it resembles the wild swans of the North. This South American bird may very likely constitute a survival of an ancient variety, which can be catalogued equally among the swans, the geese, and *Dendro cygnus*, the Whistling ducks.

Cob and pen are inordinately proud parents and take great pains to rear their small family to be as swanlike as possible. Education in feeding, swimming, flying and, most important in their early days, self-preservation, is much the same for all swanlets, though this monarch of his territory does not have to contend with the archenemy, Man.

Nevertheless, cygnets have many dangers to face: in the air, in the water, and on the ground. Birds of prey, animals, large voracious fish and, in certain areas, big turtles that reach up through the water to seize an unsuspecting baby by the leg and drag him down to drown, all take their toll. A cygnet's life is difficult until he is wise and big enough to fight his own battles. With cob and pen always on the watch his chances are good, judging by the numbers of survivors. Swans being hardy and long-lived, perhaps without their infant mortality the world might become over-populated with these large-sized birds.

These swan-geese feed almost entirely in the water, reaching down their long necks for vegetation growing on the bottom of the shallow pools and marshes they frequent. Their bills are slightly hooked at the top and are consequently unsuited for grazing, though they are able to pick up beetles, water snails, and small crustaceans. Unlike some swans, they are peaceable and tolerant not only of their fellow geese but also of the small ducks and other water birds. They would, therefore, be desirable as well as attractive as ornamental park birds.

But the Coscoroba does not take to captivity and, as a result, is rarely if ever seen away from its native continent. In 1870 a pair was placed in the London Zoological Gardens. Though the pen laid a small clutch of eggs, none hatched, owing, it is recorded, "to her excitable temper and restlessness." Later at Woburn Abbey, where the Duke of Bedford maintains a collection of exotic birds in his many-acred park, one Coscoroba nest was built. The pen managed to hatch several of her cygnet-gosling-ducklings, but only one survived. Lonely, it attached itself to the Duchess and proved an amusing and affectionate pet, though rather large and demanding. Recently in the Philadelphia Zoo a pair of these swans has managed to raise two healthy young, while the San Diego Zoo has a firmly established family.

It may seem strange to include a lowly duck in the royal family of swans. *Dendro cygnus* is not a mere duck, however, but a near relative, as his name implies. In himself, and apart from his kinship, he is an interesting little bird on account of his curious distribution. For the species, called either Tree or Whistling duck, occurs in relatively small numbers in diverse and disconnected places. Small groups are found in Louisiana, Mexico, South America, Africa, and India: always in tropical or subtropical localities.

Dendro cygnus is small, even for a duck, favors brown as a plumage color, has duckling feet with a low thumb and sharp claws, long legs, and broad rounded wings. But it also has a long slender neck of seventeen vertebrae (against a duck's eleven), and it holds this neck proudly erect to prove its relationship with the swans. Nonetheless, it dives like a duck, for its neck is not long enough to gather food by merely dunking.

Eggs are cream color and almost round, like those of the swan-goose. They are more numerous, however, sometimes numbering a dozen or more. Nests have been found containing as many as thirty-two eggs, but this may have been the product of two or more birds. The young look just like Coscoroba cygnets seen under a diminishing glass, with the short bodies, long necks and legs of their parents and royal relatives already well developed.

These ducks occupy much the same territory in South America as the swan-goose and build, as a rule, on the ground among the reeds and rushes bordering a lake or marsh. They do sometimes build in a tree but not often enough to justify the name of Tree duck. The adjective "whistling" is certainly more descriptive of them, for their wings do whistle in flight.

There is no mistaking this *Dendro cygnus*. It walks

erect and well, and it holds the head high. Upon being disturbed its voice is shrill and very unducklike. It swims laboriously and low in the water, with none of the gaiety of the duck or the power of the swan. It flies with a slow, powerful, long sweep, the wings producing a strong whirring, whining sound because of notches in the flight feathers, which allow the air to pass through. In flight the neck is stretched out and the long legs trail. Seen in silhouette, it has a definite resemblance to a swan or an immature cygnet. It constantly utters its peculiar chattering, whistling cry as it flies. This is definitely a swan habit.

Like swans, mates are deeply attached, remain faithfully together, and share family cares (the male even helps incubate, a thing which the lordly drake does not deign to do). In moments of leisure, they preen each other's feathers with all signs of affection. At dusk, when they come out to feed, they indulge in low gossipy conversation.

The name *Dendro* (pertaining to trees) and *cygnus* (swan)—in other words Tree swan—reflects the perplexity of ornithologists as to the placing of these unique little birds. They form a peculiar genus of eight species only, closely related to the Coscoroba, which stands between them and the true swans. Either it is a declining race of which only a few relics remain, or it is an aggressive new species trying to establish itself. Its curious connection with the Coscoroba swan, whose territory in South America it shares, would suggest the former.

If *Dendro cygnus* is a vanishing species that does not conform to Nature's blueprint for the future, at least it is an engaging little bird with much character. Let us hope that it will turn out to be a new and aggressive species, which will some day colonize over a wider area.

❦ 8 ❧

In Australia

THE CONTINENT of Australia has been for so long an island world that it has developed, or perhaps merely maintained, a fauna peculiar to itself. To account for its insular position, the lean black aborigines with glossy black curls have handed down their own story of the Deluge. This differs from the version of the Northern Hemisphere in that it includes no Biblical Noah with his Ark to save the favored few. In their account, some of the naked inhabitants escaped to the mountain peaks, while the laggards, caught in the rush of the waters, were changed into Black swans, possessing their own characteristics of appearance.

Modern Australians are proud of their native Black swan. It was originally placed in a genus of its own, *Chenopis*, but it is now generally associated with the genus Cygnus and named *Cygnus atratus* (swan clothed in black).

It is a true swan, lean and elegant with an exceptionally long neck, slender at the throat and thickening toward the base. When the bird is swimming, the neck is curved almost at right angles at the top, the small head and brightly polished cherry-red bill pointing stiffly downward. The plumage is midnight black, but each feather is fringed with slate gray. This produces a moiré effect. There is a distinct white band across the tip of the rather broad bill. The eye is ruby red. The wings are true swan wings, wide and strong, and the primaries, the long flight feathers, are startlingly white. Strangest of all, in a bird renowned for its swift flight, are the curled feathers on the back. These stand up in serrated rows as the bird swims, etched in silhouette against the pale water. To complete the picture perhaps the feet ought to be red, but they are slate gray, almost black.

This is the majestic cob. The pen is slightly smaller with a shorter neck, but the difference is apparent only when they are seen together. These birds seem proud of their distinctive ruffled secondaries, for they are normally seen swimming with the wings stiffly busked, the white primaries held low and very conspicuous.

The neck of the Black swan is hung even lower than that of the white swans, and the water sometimes ripples between it and the raised wings during speedy swimming.

Cygnets, when small, are very like their northern cousins in shape, and they too are of a very light brownish gray, shading to creamy white below. The feet and bill are black.

The plumage darkens very slowly and, when the bird is fully grown though not actually mature, presents a mottled appearance, each dark feather fringed with the original lighter color.

In the very early days these swans were exceedingly common over the length and breadth of the temperate zone of the Australian continent. They were also native to the adjacent island of Tasmania. During the settling of the country their numbers dwindled so alarmingly that they were considered extremely rare. Now, happily, they have responded to protection and are reappearing even in districts where they were once exterminated. Really, protection is slight, but it is enforced less by law than by a strong public sentiment, which is the best security of all.

The Black swan in a wild state is at home both on the sea and on inland rivers and lakes. It is, perhaps, the only member of the family that frequents open salt-water bays and inlets and consorts with sea gulls. They cruise in flotillas along the shore. On the ground they are the ungainliest of all swans.

In the breeding season the birds fly inland and mass in great herds on the still waters of the lonelier lakes where scores of their huge, strongly built nests may be seen dotted over a small area of swampland and shallow lagoons. For a nesting site they prefer a low island in a lake where material for nest building is available. In the absence of an actual island they construct one of their own, weaving it of branches broken from the surrounding trees. On that they will build the true nest which is always exceptionally strong and well designed, thick-walled and high. These precautions protect the cygnets from their arch-enemy, an imported fox (*vulpes vulpes*). Nests too close to the shore or exposed as a result of falling water levels are constantly invaded by this pest. A large water rat occasionally preys on the very young cygnets if they stray from their parents' surveillance.

Four to seven eggs constitute the usual clutch, though nests have been found containing as many as nine. The eggs are pale green and strangely lustrous. They are hatched in our boreal winter or fall, from late August right up to Christmas. Black swans are the fiercest and most unapproachable of swans, especially at this time. The cob undertakes part of the incubating, and both parents are devoted to their light-colored cygnets, which look like changelings as they follow their sable-clad parents.

These powerful, indomitable birds are said to have another enemy, which will attack not only the young but the adults as well. Stories from the interior relate that swan families are actually obliged to move from nesting sites to escape the persecution of the tremendous wedge-tailed eagle (*uroaetus audax*). This eagle is entirely black in its adult stage, except for a rufous streaked nape. It almost parallels the white-tailed sea eagle, the nemesis of the Whooper swan. One of the largest eagles on earth, its wing span is usually around six feet six inches, but it has been measured at seven feet and three inches and, in one case (of a bird from Tasmania), nine feet and four inches. Though this immense eagle is mainly a scavenger, it has been known to kill young emus and rabbits and baby lambs. Local stories of its predations persist despite the denials of ornithologists.

The early settlers hunted the Black swan almost to extinction though its flesh is now considered too rank for human use. The aborigines of West Australia have always used its eggs for food and still do to a large extent. They also kill the birds during the molting season as the Eskimos of the North do. This keeps the swan population within limits in Australia whereas in New Zealand, where they were introduced some years ago, they are unmolested and their increasing numbers are creating a problem. Nature, if allowed, can usually take care of such a situation. In Australia, for instance, no eggs are hatched during a prolonged dry season when the lakes and lagoons are low. Sometimes the swans refrain from nesting at all until the water with its necessary green vegetation returns. This check on disastrous increase is not the case where the birds are introduced to alien surroundings or are artificially fed.

This strange swan is, like all its kind, swift in flight. The sight and sound of a "wing" of Black swans on migration is unforgettable. The whole air is darkened as they surge past like a squadron of black aircraft in formation two by two, sounding their musical trumpeting as they go. This cry is high-pitched and has been described as resembling a tin trumpet. But there is nothing tinny about any swan's note. The cry of the Black swan is modulated and includes a great variety of notes, though it does not have the mellow resonance peculiar to the northern swans. Its appearance on the wing is exciting: a jet-black silhouette with long thin neck outstretched and sweeping pinions strikingly tipped with white. The wings produce a drumming noise, not unlike the throb of the Mute, but louder and more sustained.

Migration does not carry them far, merely from their inland nesting sites to the seacoast. There they spend the winter in the company of hosts of sea gulls and with them swim out to greet the incoming liners and escort them into harbor. This is a great feature of the seaport of Perth, West Australia, which is formed by the wide estuary of the Swan River on which the birds were first seen and recorded.

Chenopis atrata, as it was then called. was the first Australian bird to be imported to Europe. Rumors of the

existence of a fabulous black swanlike bird had drifted in from the newly discovered continent, but it was not until 1697 that the birds were seen by Europeans. In January of that year the Dutch navigator, Willem van Vlaming, anchored his ship in the estuary of a wide Australian river and sent out an exploring party in several small boats. You may imagine the amazement of these Dutchmen at the sight of a number of unbelievably black, long-necked birds. Could they possibly be swans? In these strange antipodes, where the natural order of things seemed reversed, they might be no more than the dark shadows of the familiar white swans of the North. The boats gave chase, and four of the birds were captured alive with much squawking and flailing of their powerful wings.

The ship conveyed them to Batavia, the capital of the Dutch East Indies, where the inhabitants were mystified by their appearance. In due time, news of the discovery reached Amsterdam where the Burgomeister, a naturalist, relayed the details to the Royal Society of London. It was then that the bird was named not Cygnus but *Chenopis atrata*, "a goose clothed in black." It was some years before it was included among the true swans.

These Black swans were not really popular in Europe until the Empress Josephine established a number of them in her small park at Malmaison, outside of Paris. The mad King Ludwig of Bavaria also maintained a few on a lake at his castle of Nymphenburg, and it soon became fashionable to have a pair of the ebony birds to offset the snowy Mutes. In Australia now the Mutes are imported as a contrast to the native variety. This is not always a successful experiment, for *Chenopis atrata* is neither good-tempered nor cooperative and always dominates an imported species.

Black swans in captivity now breed freely in Europe and

America. They will wander if not penned or pinioned, but they have never established themselves in a wild or even semiwild state. They are extremely decorative when associated with the white swans. Yet they have never become popular in England, where they are considered unlucky, although Sir Winston Churchill kept a few on his estate at Chartwell.

Recently a pair was dispatched by airplane to Tokyo, destined for the pool in the Imperial Palace gardens. The stewardess was busy during the entire trip feeding the birds, which ate eight pounds of wheat during the journey. A current newspaper account later mentioned "crow-watching" as having been added to the duties of the Imperial Guards. The swans had laid four eggs and the guards were assigned to keep crows from breaking and eating them.

If kept apart from other swans these Blacks will nest and hatch their eggs where only a small amount of water is available. When they are transplanted their timing is confused and often as not they bring out a batch of luckless youngsters in midwinter. Black swan cygnets, even in their native haunts, are more delicate than white swan babies and do not always survive harsh conditions. It is considered wise to remove the eggs entirely when laid at the wrong season.

West Australia, the original home of the Black swan, early proclaimed it the emblem of the territory. It became familiar to the world on the first West Australian postage stamp, issued in 1854, which depicted the swan. In this representation the bird had an exceedingly short body so as to fit into the cramped oblong. An authentic reproduction of the original stamp was issued in 1954 to commemorate the centenary of this flourishing Dominion.

These magnificent birds also appear on the arms of the seaport of Perth: two swans support a shield and crenelated crown, wings raised, each neck bearing a similar crown. The motto of the city is *Floreat*, while that of the territory is *Cygnus insignia*.

✥ 9 ✥

Myth and Legend

SWAN STORIES go back to the beginning of human history where story becomes legend, legend becomes myth, and myth merges into religious belief.

In the earliest days swans were worshiped as semidivine. Among the Greeks they were held sacred to Apollo and Aphrodite. Over the continent of Europe and in parts of Asia there are recurring tales of swan-maidens, superhuman celestial beings who turned into swan or maiden at will. Their sources cannot be traced, for the further one penetrates into the past the wider grows their range and the more interwoven they become with legends of other lands.

The Valkyries of Wagnerian opera were originally swan-maidens said to ride in groups of nine—a divine number in the Orient. They guarded heroes in battle and in death carried them to Valhalla, the Nordic heaven, familiar to us through the Nibelungen saga. Earlier the legend is found in the Vedic hymns of ancient India, where similar maidens who appeared as cirrus clouds were really "swans swimming in the blue lake of Heaven." In time of battle they descended as winged guardians to rescue the favored hero and carry him to the Vedic heaven. They too appeared in groups of nine. These Vedic Valkyries wore swan wings and were semi-divine, possessing extraordinary powers. Later on the white swan wings were adapted to adorn the angels of the Christian church. As time passed they were painted gold and red and blue but remained essentially the wings of swans.

This early belief in supernatural guardians led eventually to stories of swan-women who had lost their divine attributes and retained only the power of transforming themselves into birds. All over Europe—particularly in Scandinavia, and in England, Wales, and Ireland—these lovely young creatures were said to be seen bathing in lakes and mountain tarns, their magic "shifts" laid carelessly by on the grassy banks. A man enamored of their beauty who, with luck and sleight of hand, managed to steal one of the feathered garments could claim the maiden for his wife—though she seems to have had none of the true swan's faithfulness and devotion. If ever she found her "shift" again, even after many years as an apparently happy wife and mother, she would hastily don it and be up and away with never a backward look. The obtuse husband seems never to have destroyed the fatal apparel. He just put it up in the attic or stowed it away with

the winter blankets. Therefore after many years he would
be left with his disappointment and a brood of swan-children
on his hands.

These later swan-maidens always possessed a feathered
garment in which lay their power of transformation as well
as the gift of eternal youth. In earlier swan stories a veil or
more often a golden chain carried the charm, and the swan-
maiden was born with the magic chain around her neck.
Sagas too numerous to mention developed this story, and

various versions were popular not only in the northern countries but throughout the Old World wherever swans were to
be found. In most accounts the children inherited their swan-
natures from a swan-mother, but they did not always have
the power to change themselves into birds at will.

It is in Ireland that the legendary swan-maidens are said
to be seen to this day by those capable of recognizing them.
The Irish version of the legend was probably derived from
the lovely Bewick's swan rather than from the stately Mute,
which is far from common in the Emerald Isle.

A tale runs that in the time of St. Patrick, around A.D.
420, Lir was king of the Irish Dana, the fabulous Tuatha de
Danann. He and his beautiful wife, Aobh, had four children:
Fionala, Conny, Fiachna, and Huw. The mother died when
they were still young, and Lir imprudently married her sister,
Aoife, a sorceress. Aoife was insanely jealous of her step-
children because of their beauty and their lovely singing
voices. In a fit of passion she turned them into swans, allowing them to retain their reasoning power and exquisite song.
She decreed that they must keep the form of swans for nine
hundred years, one third to be spent on Lake Derry, one third
on Enis Berg, and the remainder on the Mull of Kintyre.

Great stress is laid on their singing. Perhaps this signifies
that the *Cygnus musica* inspired the story rather than the
Bewick's. At the end of the enchanted nine centuries they
were captured by a prince who threw golden chains around
their necks. Thereupon they were changed into incredibly
old people and died.

In another story, a virtuous swan-mother, the faithful
wife of an unappreciative king, died in giving birth to seven
swan-children. The paternal grandmother, who had always
hated her mysteriously beautiful daughter-in-law, ordered a
servant to kill the seven children. Because they were innocent

and beguiling, he could not nerve himself to obey. When the grandmother found them still alive, she commissioned a tougher menial to dispatch them and to bring back to her the seven necklaces as proof of his deed. He too weakened, but he persuaded the children to remove their necklaces—whereupon, to his surprise and probably to their own as well, they all turned into swans and flew away.

These stories have appeared and reappeared in varying forms. Some end happily with the children regaining their talismans and returning to confront the wicked stepmother. In others they are saved by one of them who escapes the transformation, as in the case of Eliza and the eleven swans. In the Hans Christian Andersen story the charm was irrevocably lost, so Eliza wove each swan brother a coat of stinging nettles and thus restored his manly form. This prickly weed was regarded as a magic herb, as was the sedge, cotton grass (*Eriophorum*), and the beautiful little star grass (*Hypoziz*).

Urtica
Stinging Nettle

Myth and Legend

Among the Mongolian Buriat tribes living around the shores of Lake Baikal there is an interesting variant of the tale in which the husband returned the swan garment to his wife when she begged for it, after their marriage had produced eleven sons and six daughters. With no hesitation she donned it and flew off, crying into the air: "Ye are earthly beings and remain on earth. I am from heaven and fly back home!" One of her daughters tried to hinder her by grasping her feet with sooty hands—hence the swan's black feet. This may have been inspired by a Jankowski, whose feet truly are sooty black.

The swan-knight legend is a later variant of the story. In the earliest version only one of seven regains his human form. His swan-brothers are harnessed to a boat in which he invariably arrives in the nick of time to rescue some oppressed maiden.

The first written account came from France and concerned an ancestor of Godfrey de Bouillon, Chevalier du Cygne. It relates that King Lothair, ruler of a country near Hungary, lost his way while hunting and met a strange and beautiful maiden called Eloise. She was a swan-maiden, and of course he married her. Equally of course, she died giving birth to seven children, six boys and a girl. The wicked stepmother evidently knew all about swan-children, for she removed their necklaces, with the usual result—though the little swan princess in some way eluded her. Five of the brothers contrived to recover their magic chains, but the gold of the other son's chain had been melted down and made into a goblet. Having to remain a swan, he drew the boat for his older brother, Helyas, who in time married a noble lady, Beatrice de Bouillon. He thus became the remote ancestor of the celebrated Chevalier du Cygne.

The brother who remained a swan seems to have had a

hard time. In one medieval woodcut from *Vergier d'Honneur*, a French account of about 1486, the tiny wizened swan is depicted with a heavy chain about his neck, straining to tow his massive brother dressed in a suit of mail, in a boat that looks like a Hudson River ferry equipped with anchor, mast, and cabin. The water is crimped in waves suggesting a mill race, and the poor little swan seems hardly able to make headway.

It became fashionable in medieval times to call oneself a Knight of the Swan. Godfrey de Bouillon was probably the first, but the best known of all was Lohengrin. All were dedicated to the assistance of damsels in distress.

A great many of the swan legends seem to have arisen among the Celtic tribes of the lower Rhine in the parts we now call Holland and Belgium. Old geological charts show this region to have been a partially submerged coast with vast lagoons and marshes particularly suited to swans. Their coming and going on migration coincided with the vernal and autumnal equinoxes, and they were in consequence considered the messengers of the god of light and warmth and growth. As the earliest and the most spectacular of the migratory birds, swans appeared in the early spring as harbinger of the god's return, and they departed with him in the fall. Hence primitive imagination endowed these birds with supernatural qualities.

In the lake-studded domain of the Elector of Brandenburg the Order of the Swan was inaugurated in 1440. This was a philanthropic, religious association of carefully selected princes and nobles. It lapsed after many years but was revived in 1843, open to men of all creeds for "the amelioration of physical and moral ills."

The swan has always been a symbol of nobility. In 1304, when Edward I of England was knighted, he swore an oath on two swans, and Edward III flaunted a swan badge which carried the motto, "Hay, Hay, thou white swan, by Godde's soul I am thy Man." Swans also appear in heraldry, and the crest of the de Bohun family (Mary de Bohun became the wife of Henry IV) depicts a swan wearing a royal crown around its neck, with a trailing leash.

But long, long before this the Greeks had honored the swan. To them it was a bird of wisdom as well as prophecy and was also connected with music. In the hymn of Kallimarchus the clouds were singing swans who seven times circled Delos at the birth of Phoebus Apollo, who in later years fixed the seven notes of the musical scale that took the place of the five-tone scale then in use.

Swans appear in the story of Phaeton, the intrepid son of Helios, who was burned to death when recklessly driving the chariot of the Sun. His friend, Cygnus, was inconsolable. He woefully haunted the river into which the charred body had fallen. Apollo, in pity, turned him into a swan and afterward placed him among the stars as the constellation Cygnus. This Cygnus, a son of Poseidon, had been rejected by his mother and cared for by a swan, until a fisherman found and adopted him.

Swans appear often in Greek mythology, always in connection with the gods. They were, no doubt, common in ancient Greece and, according to Socrates, they were not always the Mutes. In Plato's *Phaedo* there occurs a memorable passage which suggests a Whooper or perhaps a Bewick's. In the Athens prison where the condemned Socrates was to drink poisoned hemlock, his friends argued about death and the future life. Socrates, calm and cheerful, laughed at them gently and said:

> It seems I appear to you so less prophetic than the swans who, when they perceive that they must die, though they have been used to singing before, sing then more than ever, rejoicing that they are about to depart to that deity whose servants they are. But men through their own fear of death say the swans are lamenting, singing their last song through grief. . . . It is my view that swans sing not because they are sad but because they belong to Apollo and, knowing what happiness they will have in the next world, rejoice on that last day more excellently than at any preceding time. I am like the swans. I also belong to Apollo, and he has made me as clear-sighted as the birds, so that I depart this life in no less spirits than they.

Proceeding eastward from the Isles of Greece, the swan is reported as dangerous, even vindictive. Among the Shamans of Eastern Asia it was declared that dire misfortune would result from killing or even molesting a swan. And the Buriats tell how a swan whose nest had been destroyed flew over and dropped a burning brand upon the house of the guilty one. Thereupon the whole village was burned to the ground.

Myth and Legend

The natives of that region offered prayers to the spirit of the Siberian swan, the small Jankowski, named by them the Sen or Khun.

Jankowski was possibly the species of wild swan that figured in the "Awakening to Pain" of Gautama Buddha. Prince Siddartha was born about 600 B.C., the son of a king of the Sakyas, a warrior race settled in the foothills of the Himalayas in a district now known as Behar. The king hoped to bring to naught a prophecy that his son and heir would one day choose the life of a wandering monk seeking solace for the sorrows of the world. He walled the palace garden against pain and death.

One day when the young prince was playing there with his cousin, Devadetta, a flight of wild swans passed low overhead. Devadetta, loosing an impulsive arrow, wounded the leader, which fell at Siddartha's feet. The prince gathered the wounded bird in his arms and tenderly removed the painful dart, marveling that the "godlike speed which throbbed in that white wing" could be so suddenly stilled.

Thus began the Quest, which led to the Great Renunciation and culminated in the teaching that has swayed the minds of millions.

This story proves the presence of swans in the Northern India of that time. As the crow flies, the kingdom of Behar lies not too far from the headwaters of the great Chinese rivers, the Yangtze and the Hoang-ho. Matthew Arnold, timing the incident "on a day in Spring," states that the swans were on their way to their nesting places "on Himalaya's breast." It is possible that swans did nest on those high mountain slopes in those long-ago days.

Reverence for the swan probably stems from some forgotten knowledge of the beliefs of ancient India. In the very earliest times the swan typified a form of the Divine

Principle. In the Vedic literature of India it was referred to as "The Swan out of Time and Space." It symbolized the Spirit of God of the Hebrew Bible that moved on the face of the waters on the first day of Creation. It was also the Hamsa bird, the A-ham-sa, the refuge of the enlightened and the symbol of Divine Wisdom and Wisdom Beyond the Reach of Man. The word Hamsa actually means a wild swan, and the reverse, Asmah, has an esoteric meaning: "I Am That." It was named by sages of India the Swan out of Eternity, the Creative Aspect of Brahma, which lays the golden egg at the beginning of each Kalpa or Day of Brahm, the egg from which the new Universe will be born.

The swan in India took the place of the sacred ibis of Egypt. It could be either white or black, the two aspects of the Unknowable Deity. In the *Book of Dyzan*, the White Swan from the Starry Heights overshadowed the various stages of creation; and where in the beginning it was dual, the Great One of the Dual Force, a black swan and a white, as soon as light was created it became and remained pure white.

The character of the swan, its purity, its intelligence, its integrity, seems to have been in the thoughts of those who formulated this early cosmology. This is particularly strange because the bird is not now native to the part of India where these beliefs originated. India is a tropical and subtropical country; swans are by nature paleoarctic, immune to cold but intolerant of heat. This suggests that the religious connotation was introduced by some even earlier civilization, or at least that it was first recorded when the climate was much colder than it is now.

Most of the swan legends and myths come from northern Europe, however. The father and mother of all swans were to be found at the foot of Yggdrasil, the great ash tree that symbolized the Universe. Here the two superb white

birds swam forever on the sacred fountain of Urd, who was herself a swan-maiden and one of the Three Norns, the Fates of Nordic myth. These birds were also sacred to Niord, the Norse Neptune, just as Cygnus of Greece was said to be the son of the sea god.

The Finnish Kalevala is linked more closely with oriental myth, the Beauteous Daughter of the Ether being "overshadowed by a divine water bird" which laid seven eggs in her lap.

In Finnish legend we have the story of the sinister Great White Swan of Tuonela. The reckless magician-hero, Lemminkainen, traveled to the north country to woo the daughter of Louhi, who set him to perform certain tasks. The hero had inherited from his mother a talent for magic, and he easily captured the Giant Elk of Evil Power, Hiisi, and caught and bridled the fire-breathing horses. But the White Swan swimming on the Black River was his downfall. He was defeated and cast into the waterfall of Tuoni, the death god himself. The saga ends with this lament:

> Thus the hero Lemminkainen,
> Thus the handsome Kajkomeile,

The untiring suitor, dieth
In the River of Tuoni,
In the death realm of Manala.

In the music of Jan Sibelius' symphonic poem, "The Swan of Tuonela," the throbbing note of the Mute swan's wings is exquisitely interpreted.

In Iceland a mythical swan appears in the form of a giant Whooper floating on a lake hollowed from the black basalt side of a mountain. It bears the fate of the world in its strong black and yellow bill. When it drops the ring it

has been holding for ages untold, the result of the atom bomb would be that of a firecracker compared to the damage which the ring will do. The entire world, it is prophesied, will disintegrate on the instant.

Swans are used in pure design and frequently appear in heraldry. It is difficult to portray them as birds rather than as just graceful pottery design. A swan is never portrayed on an Egyptian mural or bas-relief, whereas such birds as the ibis and the heron are faithfully represented, and their breeds of ducks can be recognized to this day. The swan is not native to Africa, but surely a few of them must have ventured into the delectable papyrus-bordered Nile. It is curious that the Egyptian artists with their eye for decorative form would have omitted the graceful swan from their wall paintings of water birds without conscious reason. A lifelike delineation does appear among their hieroglyphs, but it has the phonetic value of *hetem* (to destroy, or the destroyer). Why was it so named? An explanation may possibly be found in

the Book of Leviticus, where the swan is three times condemned as unclean and therefore unfit for human food. The
Laws of this document were, of course, derived from the
Egyptians, and the meat of the swan, which is rather gamy
and rich, may have been considered unsuitable to that climate
and the climate of the Promised Land.

Poets as well as metaphysicians, musicians, and artists
have been inspired by these elusive birds floating upon a
reflected image on the still waters. The first known lyric
in the English language with a bird as its subject dates back
to the eighth century. Cynewulf wove his runic signature
into the text, thus establishing his authorship. The manuscript
is part of a collection entitled *The Exeter Book Riddle*, and
the music of the swan's wings is graphically described in a
translation by Tyndall:

> My robe is noiseless when I tread the earth
> Or tarry neath the banks or stir the shadows;
> But when these shining wings, this depth of air
> Bear me aloft above the bending shores
> Where men abide, and far the Welkin's strength
> Over the multitude conveys me, then
> With rushing whir and clear melodious sound
> My raiment sings. And like a wandering spirit
> I float unweariedly o'er flood and field.

A later madrigal, one of those ancient English unaccom-
panied part songs so beloved of glee singers, refers to the
swan's death song:

> The silver swan that living had no note,
> When death appeared unlocked her silver throat,
> Leaning her breast against the reedy shore,
> Thus sang her first and last and sung no more.

Many poets have elaborated on this theme, the swan voiceless
in life and articulate only at the time of death.

Myth and Legend

Memorable descriptions of swans have come down to us, as in Milton's *Paradise Lost* (VII, 438):

> . . . the swan with Archéd neck
> Between her white wings mantling proudly, rows
> Her state with oarie feet: yet oft they quit
> The dank, and rising on stiff pennons, tow'r
> The mid Aereal Sky . . .

Keats, the great painter of lyric word pictures, gave us this portrait:

> There saw the swan his neck of archéd snow,
> And oared himself along in majesty,
> Sparkled his jetty eye; his feet did show
> Beneath the waves like Afric's ebony.

The poet Yeats, looking out upon the nine-and-fifty wild swans at Coole in Ireland, as they floated on the brimming waters of the lake under a gray October sky, was inspired to write one of his loveliest poems which closed with these lines:

> But now they drift on the still water,
> Mysterious, beautiful;
> Among what rushes will they build,
> By what lake's edge or pool
> Delight men's eyes when I awake one day
> To find that they have flown away?

◦ᔈ 10 ᔆ◦

Care and Keeping of Swans

OF ALL WATER BIRDS swans are certainly the most ornamental and interesting. The raising and breeding of a pair of swans on one's own property can be a most rewarding hobby. All that is required is protected water, adequate vegetation, and an understanding of swan needs. If wisely cared for they will breed regularly year after year and raise their charming families without difficulty on your part. If they ever grow too numerous for your restricted place, there is always a market for healthy young swans.

Care and Keeping of Swans

Swan-keeping on small estates is becoming increasingly popular, and I am hoping that those who have read these pages will be inspired to make a closer acquaintance with these beautiful birds.

A pair can be purchased at no great expense, and a small sheet of water, clean and fresh with, if possible, natural vegetation, will suffice for them. They are a purely aquatic species. They live and breed on the water, and the joy of keeping them lies largely in their dignified beauty as they swim reflected feather by feather against a background of dark trees. It must be remembered that a swan, even a semi-domesticated Mute, is primarily a wild bird, and in his wildness lies his charm. He may become friendly if well treated, but he will never be docile like a goose or a duck.

A large part of the scanty information on the care of swans is inaccurate if not actually harmful, especially when it is disseminated by breeders who are obliged to keep their birds penned and are anxious to sell them as quickly as possible. Swans, particularly the Mute, are healthy and very hardy. Under proper conditions they ought to enjoy a life span of up to seventy years, but few captives survive beyond five or seven years. This shortening of their existence is usually caused by a lack of their keeper's understanding.

At the time of purchasing swans, even from a recommended dealer, remember that they do not mature until they are at least three years old. They cannot be expected to mate until the following year. Most buyers are in a hurry to start a swannery and demand swans of breeding age, but only rarely do they get what they are seeking. Owing to feeding requirements and the fighting instinct natural to swans, it is not profitable for dealers to care for them long enough for them to reach the breeding age. Therefore few breeders are for sale.

So be content to buy a pair of young ones and wait for them to settle down in their new home before they start the serious business of raising a family. They are just as ornamental at an early age, and they are more easily tamed, especially if there are no others of their kind to irritate them.

Some time before your swans are delivered, look to the pond on which they are to live. Be sure there is an abundance of pond weed. If there is not enough, it is wise to plant some at least a year in advance so that it can be well established before your swans start feeding on it. If your pond is literally choked with water weeds, your swans will soon prune them and keep them within bounds without destroying them. So be lavish. Swans are skilled pruners, eating the roots where they are too thick and nibbling the superfluous topping. Plant also reeds and rushes, wild celery and iris, and other ornamental plants to provide privacy and shelter as well as sustenance. Make your pond a luxurious place.

Right away, as soon as you have launched your swans on their pond, *feed* them, for bought swans are often, indeed usually, lamentably semistarved.

If there is no abundance of greenery you must provide extra food. Grass clippings are the best substitute for water plants, for they contain vitamins and minerals. Lettuce, celery, and cabbage trimmings can be procured in bulk from your grocer, but they ought to be used only as a substitute, not as the main diet. Such foods provide roughage and bulk, but good results cannot be expected from a year-round feeding of grocery discards. In any case, all green stuff must be thrown into the edge of the water and not deposited on the bare ground. A swan will not, really cannot, "stubble" like a goose, for its bill is not shaped for this task.

Proper feeding cannot be too strongly emphasized. Feathers can effectively hide an emaciated body, and a swan is a

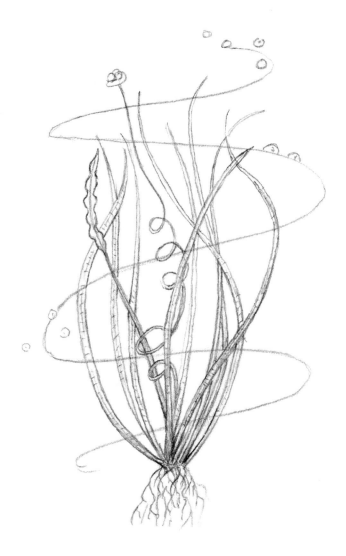

Wild Celery

real die-hard. He will live uncomplainingly on his own fat until he collapses and expires from malnutrition. He cannot tell you he is hungry as a dog might, but will just suffer in silence and mysteriously die. So see that you buy a young and healthy pair, feed them well, and do not expect too much of them for the first year or two. They will repay you for your consideration as the years go on.

If, instead of starting on a domain of their own, they must share a stretch of water with other and fully grown swans already in possession, there is sure to be some trouble. These novices, encountering unnatural conditions for the first time, will find it difficult to adjust to other birds. The established birds will resent their intrusion and chase them around. They will also prevent the newcomers from getting a fair share of food at this time when they need it most.

So stretch a wire barrier between the new ones and the others until they are acclimatized and able to hold their own. It is most important under these circumstances to see that they are getting their fair share of the food. If they are separated for a few months they will become acquainted without emotional disturbance. A collection of young birds will usually get along pretty well. Black swans, even when young, will dominate, however. Even the powerful Mute must be protected in their company.

If there are merely ducks in the pond, extra rations for the swans can be placed in a bucket half filled with water and fastened to a stake in the water high enough to be out of reach of the smaller birds. Even if the pond is lush with weeds, provide a little grain every twenty-four hours.

Grain is a supplementary food only, and it should be a blend of three or four different kinds, cracked corn, wheat, oats, and rye, which will supply a bigger assortment of vitamins than any one grain alone. Swans require a variety of vitamins just as chickens, dogs, and people do.

Care and Keeping of Swans

If you want your swans to breed—and who does not look forward to seeing a flotilla of cygnets?—you must not expect them to do so in a crowded community. A quiet retreat must be provided at nesting time where the other birds cannot disturb or molest them. Always remember that a swan is a wild bird and at this time is definitely nongregarious. On a large lake swans will find a safe spot for themselves and defend it gallantly, but on a smaller, more public area they cannot do this. If there are no tall rushes a shelter must be provided; even a large-size carton open at one side will do.

Do not be deceived into thinking that all you have to do is to buy a pair of swans and let them manage for themselves. Their environment, their diet may not please them at first. They may not even please each other, for in the wild they could choose a mate. But care and kindness, combined with quiet, will usually produce the desired result, even after a few failures. The birds may mate happily, they may build a nest, and the pen may lay her quota of eggs and faithfully incubate them, with no success. Do not be discouraged if this happens. Look again to their diet and their environment, and next year all may be well. Once a bird begins to lay it will usually continue year after year for twenty-five years or more, even if the first eggs fail to hatch.

Elodea

{ 154 }

Watch them. If they leave the water too frequently and wander around on the shore they are usually hungry, for they will not do this except under stress. Their feet get very sore if they walk too much. If they do this, feed them grain and more greens on the water, but do not feed them bread. It is not a good food for them and does not take the place of fresh greens.

Swans do not require as much food in winter as in summer and spring. If you feed an unlimited amount in September and October, they will then lose their appetites and require very little during the colder months. This is, of course, Nature's provision for the period when food is scarce in the wild, when icing makes it hard for them to feed in the water. In·very severe weather they can be brought into a barn or shelter, but the cold does not seem to bother them as long as sufficient food is available.

Allow your swans as much freedom as possible, for their independence is part of their charm. Permit them to preserve their own beautiful dignity and pride. Above all, do not raise their cygnets in a brooder if you want healthy and knowledgeable birds. Swans are exemplary parents, and the cygnets have much to learn from them.

Avoid buying hand- or brooder-raised swans in the first place. These have been kept as a rule on dry land and have been fed a quantity of wet mash without sufficient compensating greens. No one can hope to raise strong and healthy birds under such conditions. Moreover, hand-raised swans tend to be too tame. They have not learned the hard facts of life or the natural wariness that their parents would have been careful to inculcate. They need to be taught the meaning of fear, which they will not learn in a brooder. Allow the pen and her mate the cob to attend to their education in every detail. Do not try to restrict them in any way. There is a great deal that a swan must learn if he is to be true to his heritage.

In order to keep your new swans happily at home on their lake or pond, their wings should have been properly clipped or pinioned. If this has not been done, attend to it at once, for if the birds are able to fly away they will get lost, bewildered in a strange region, and the chances are that they will not survive.

Yearling or older swans will probably have had their wings clipped to prevent escape; they may even have been pinioned. If they are merely clipped, this process must be repeated year after year, for they annually molt their big flight feathers. Cutting the wing feathers is a more or less simple business, if you are able to handle the bird. You merely clip ten or twelve inches off the first six primary feathers on one wing. This makes it difficult for the bird to fly in a straight line.

Pinioning is permanent and more satisfactory, and should be done when the cygnets are only ten to fourteen days old. To do this take a small pair of scissors and cut off the last joint of one wing, being careful not to cut the pinlike part of the second joint. It ought not to bleed much, and many times not at all. If it does bleed, it will be only a few drops and will last only a minute, so no medication is necessary. It is just as easy as cutting a string for, at this age, the wing is very small. Pinioning a young swan is not cruel; indeed it would be cruel not to pinion it. If the bird is fully grown, however, it is wise to have a certified veterinarian to do the job.

The type of bird you wish to raise depends on your taste and ambitions. The Mute swan has always been the favorite. It is considered the handsomest and is certainly the most conscious of its obligations to show off. It is also the easiest to domesticate, as it is not so prone to wander as are the

Zannichellia Palustris

Potamogetan

{ 158 }

more migratory birds. It is, however, inclined to boss the lake. Many people now prefer the hybrid Polish swan, a cross between the Royal and the closely related Immutable, a smaller and usually a gentler bird. This hybrid Polish swan deviates from both its kin in having yellowish legs instead of pink or black, but on the water it is difficult to distinguish from the beautiful Mute. It is just as regal and has its cousin's lovely habit of swimming with neck curved and wings held high. Many of the swans now seen in our parks are these hybrids.

A great advantage from the point of view of the dealer is the fact that at the first molt the feathers of the Polish swans come in pure white, so that it is difficult for the novice to determine the age of the birds. Consequently a yearling can be sold as a two- or three-year-old breeder. It is wise to purchase a young bird knowingly and give it time to grow. A pair of Polish swans can be bought for about a hundred dollars, and they have the advantage of maturing at an earlier age than the larger Royal.

If your pond is small and you want to be different, you may choose the charming little Black-neck. The initial price is high—nearly four hundred dollars for a young pair—and they are considered by some delicate and hard to raise.

The Black-neck is gentle, friendly, and particularly ornamental on the water. It is very suitable for smaller domains and will live happily on a small pool. But it is sensitive to cold and is often muddled by the change of hemisphere and the sequence of seasons, so that even in its native land it is decreasing alarmingly. By experimenting with keeping and breeding this little swan, you may be helping to preserve an interesting species in danger of extinction.

A little Black-neck of my acquaintance was bought at the early age of eight months and brought up by hand, in a

park near San Jose, California. He was free to wander at
will and would meet visitors at the entrance of the public
grounds and conduct them around the lake, waddling along
and talking incessantly with an extraordinary command of
swan vocabulary. His mate was shy and remained on the
water, a beautiful sight swimming with her black neck and
pure white body reflected as in a mirror. These swans were
living amicably with a pair of Polish, for they had all been
brought up together from the cygnet stage. Later little Fin-
negan and his spouse were transferred to the local zoo through
no fault of his own or his companion swan, but because the
public took advantage of his innocent friendliness. One
man even offered him a lighted cigarette to eat! If he had
been raised in the wild by a pen and a cob, he would have
known how to protect himself and would have mistrusted
the genus *homo sapiens*.

Because the Black-neck is difficult to import and ex-
pensive to procure, it is rarely seen except in zoological gardens. The Black swan from Australia is different. It is

prolific, anything but shy, and actually seems to enjoy captivity. It will even settle down in an enclosure with only drinking water available. It would, however, defeat your ends to keep it thus for it is exceedingly clumsy on land, while in the water it is one of the most beautiful of all swans, lean, dignified, with an air of pride and race. Black swans are frequently seen associated with the pure white Mutes or Polish, and the contrast of black and white birds is striking. It must be remembered, however, that the Blacks will dominate if allowed to do so. It is best to get them when they are young and condition them by bringing them up with the older birds. I have seen them consorting with other species where all was peace, but in every case they had been introduced as half-grown cygnets.

During nesting time the Blacks must have a penned-off retreat entirely to themselves, or there will be trouble however meek they seem to have become.

The keeping of Black swans carries a certain distinction. Where the Royal or Mute is queenly, the Black is definitely a prince. With his long slender neck, the curled and ruffled jet feathers on his back, and his swift propulsion on the water, he seems to outdistance anything on the lake. The vivid red of his bill makes him a strikingly handsome bird.

Although permits are not needed to own foreign swans, at the present time neither of the two native species controlled by the U.S. Fish and Wildlife Service may be privately owned. In any event, the Whistler and the Trumpeter are not recommended as lake birds. They are unhappy if confined and very averse to breeding in captivity. You may see specimens of the Whistler on display in many zoological gardens, but they are considered merely show pieces and are unstatisfactory for breeding purposes. Best leave these untamed birds to the freedom of their native wilds.

This applies to the Whooper and the Bewick's swans as well. I believe I can safely assert that you will never see a Bewick's on a public lake, though Peter Scott is successfully raising them on his Wildfowl Trust at Slimbridge in Gloucestershire, England. As for a Trumpeter, I do not know a single one in captivity unless it is a salvaged cripple.

If you ever find a Whistler or a Trumpeter that has been wounded, report it at once to your local Fish and Game Department. Then, if they will allow you to do so, take it into your care just for its beautiful sake. It may settle down and be happy with you, but even if you find it a mate it is doubtful whether it will raise a family.

The Coscoroba swan is a challenge to the really ambitious. Cygnets can sometimes be purchased from the San Diego Zoo or the Philadelphia Zoo, and it would be wise to start with healthy zoo-raised babies. Ordinary dealers do not care to invest in this exotic breed, and importing them from their native land would, no doubt, be very costly and unprofitable. Even if they survived the journey they would be handicapped by the change of climate.

If you decide to be very valiant, procure a pair recommended by the curator of a zoo and bring them up according to his instructions. Cold will be their enemy, for they usually persist in nesting at the end of January. The young will hatch out in the bleak, chilly days of February, when there is severe weather in some localities. In a cold climate of course a good shelter must be provided, as well as plenty of extra food—green stuff and grain—and the water must be kept open for them as much as possible. It is encouraging that Coscorobas have been raised in the Philadelphia Zoo, where the winters are extremely bleak.

If successful you will have the immense satisfaction of propagating a most interesting and unusual bird. The cygnets will be a delight, vividly marked and individual in personality.

As with any kind of pet, swans need care and understanding, but they are a hardy race and, once established under suitable conditions, will prosper and be an unending joy.

ABOUT THE AUTHOR

LILLIAN GRACE PACA has published four previous books about birds and aquatic animals, including *Introduction to Western Birds* and *Sea-gulls and Such*. She has drawn and painted hundreds of bird studies and, for four years, wrote and illustrated a popular newspaper column on the subject. Born in Jamaica, where her father was a British Army career officer, she is a naturalized United States citizen and a resident of Pacific Grove, California.